SA(Y

PRAISE

COMPENDIU

MAGICAL THINGS

"Radleigh Valentine will take you on a fun and fabulous tour to explore the many ways we can dialogue with the Divine. A must-read for beginners and those just peeking out of the mystical closet as well as die-hards who want a reference guide to everything from angels and faeries to divination tools, meditation, and mantras— all in one magical place! Hop on for the ride of your life."

— **Colette Baron-Reid**, spiritual intuitive, founder of Oracle School, and author of many best-selling oracle decks and books

"I love this book. If you could choose only one book to activate magic in your life, this should be it! You will soar into the stars with Radleigh Valentine's excellent advice and wisdom, offered in practical, easy-to-understand ways. This lovely tome is filled with grace and love from an author who truly understands the mystical path. Highly recommended!"

— **Denise Linn**, author of *Energy Strands: The Ultimate Guide to Clearing the Cords That Are Constricting Your Life*

"In this masterpiece, Radleigh Valentine collects his inspired insights on every major tool I've ever heard of to help make your life a dream come true—the way it's meant to be. This is an absolute must-have in every home library."

— **Mike Dooley**, *New York Times* best-selling author of *Infinite Possibilities*

"Compendium of Magical Things provides readers with delightful step-by-step instructions for deciphering the language of the Divine. Even better, its magical author Radleigh Valentine teaches you how to bring more wonder and fun into your life. Whether you relate to angels, synchronicity, tarot cards, runes, or other oracles—or just want to learn how to have an intimate conversation with Source energy—it's all here and presented in a most irresistible way. Read this book!"

— **Christiane Northrup, M.D.**, *New York Times* best-selling author of *Goddesses Never Age*

"No matter what room Radleigh Valentine walks into, he lights it up. He really does live a magical life and has the incredible gift of showing others how they can too. He distills this knowledge in his book Compendium of Magical Things, an accessible guide to tapping into your inner gifts, unlocking magic in your life, and creating your own destiny. Radleigh is a bright light to this world, and I am grateful to call him a dear friend."

— **Kyle Gray**, best-selling author of *Raise Your Vibration* and *Angel Prayers*

"*In* Compendium of Magical Things, *Radleigh Valentine has done what he does best: make complicated things easy to understand. Whether you're looking for a closer connection to your angels or ways to get answers to your prayers and meditations, you'll find all that and more in this book. Radleigh combines his poignant insights with laugh-out-loud moments, describing magical oracles in an approachable, intriguing way. Consider the Compendium your mystical field guide to the Divine!*"

— **Rebecca Campbell**, best-selling author of *Rise Sister Rise* and *Light Is the New Black*

"*Just as Radleigh Valentine delights audiences with his sparkly shoes, outfits, and personality, he manages to do the same with words. I can feel the depth of his knowledge and experience as he shares about each modality with ease and humor . . . as well as a bit of sparkly magic, Radleigh-style. The time he spends on the history and usage of each of these magical divination tools enables the reader to feel into what would be best for them—and it would make a nonbeliever a little curious! Most of all, I appreciate the organization of the material and the great attention Radleigh has given each piece of this.* Compendium of Magical Things *will be a great handbook for seekers that will stand the test of time.*"

— **Joan Ranquet**, animal communicator, author, and founder of Communication with All Life University

COMPENDIUM OF

MAGICAL
THINGS

ALSO BY RADLEIGH VALENTINE

Books

How to Be Your Own Genie

The Big Book of Angel Tarot

Card Decks

Animal Tarot Cards

Fairy Tarot Cards

Angel Answers Oracle Cards

Guardian Angel Tarot Cards

Archangel Power Tarot Cards

Angel Tarot Cards

All of the above are available online and
at your local bookstore. Please visit:

Radleigh's website: www.RadleighValentine.com
Hay House USA: www.hayhouse.com®
Hay House Australia: www.hayhouse.com.au
Hay House UK: www.hayhouse.co.uk
Hay House India: www.hayhouse.co.in

RADLEIGH VALENTINE

COMPENDIUM OF

MAG*I*CAL THINGS

COMMUNICATING WITH THE DIVINE
TO CREATE THE LIFE OF
YOUR DREAMS

HAY HOUSE, INC.

Carlsbad, California • New York City
London • Sydney • New Delhi

Copyright © 2018 by Radleigh Valentine

Published in the United States by: Hay House, Inc.: www.hayhouse.com® • **Published in Australia by:** Hay House Australia Pty. Ltd.: www.hayhouse.com .au • **Published in the United Kingdom by:** Hay House UK, Ltd.: www.hayhouse .co.uk • **Published in India by:** Hay House Publishers India: www.hayhouse .co.in

Cover design: Barbara LeVan Fisher • *Interior design:* Nick C. Welch

Figures 7.1, 7.2, and 7.3: Illustrations by Keira Rose • *Figures 9.1, 9.2, 9.3, 9.4, 9.5, and 9.6:* Courtesy of Astrolabe, Inc., www.alabe.com

The author of this book doesn't dispense medical advice or prescribe the use of any technique as a form of treatment for physical, emotional, or medical problems without the advice of a physician, either directly or indirectly. The intent of the author is only to offer information of a general nature to help you in your quest for emotional and spiritual well-being. In the event you use any of the information in this book for yourself, the author and the publisher assume no responsibility for your actions.

Library of Congress Cataloging-in-Publication Data

Names: Valentine, Radleigh, author.
Title: Compendium of magical things : communicating with the divine to create the life of your dreams / Radleigh Valentine.
Description: 1st edition. | Carlsbad, California : Hay House, Inc., [2018]
Identifiers: LCCN 2018024181| ISBN 9781401951221 (tradepaper ; alk. paper) | ISBN 9781401951238 (E-book)
Subjects: LCSH: Divination. | Spirituality. | Spiritual life.
Classification: LCC BF1773 .V35 2018 | DDC 133.3--dc23 LC record available at https://lccn.loc.gov/2018024181

Tradepaper ISBN: 978-1-4019-5122-1
e-book ISBN: 978-1-4019-5123-8

10 9 8 7 6 5 4 3 2 1
1st edition, December 2018

Printed in the United States of America

For Those Who Seek
but Refuse to Be Afraid

CONTENTS

INTRODUCTION

THE JOURNEY

I have been on a *journey*. It's been a magical, amazing, jaw-dropping, and completely awe-inspiring path I've walked these past few months. The process of writing this book showed me things and took me places I never expected.

My love of the angels, tarot, and oracle cards has meant that these divination tools have always been all I needed to commune with the Divine, get the answers I sought, and manifest a magical life. Therefore, I hadn't pursued most of the other ways we can communicate with the Divine and allow magic to enter into our lives. Writing this book changed all that. I've learned things about myself that were completely hidden from me, and I'm so very grateful for the insights. My eyes were opened to the wonders to be explored by using other types of oracles and other languages of the Divine, and I've loved every minute.

You may be asking yourself why you'd even want to communicate with the Divine anyway. Well, when you connect actively and freely with the Universe, magical things can start to happen in your life. Guidance comes to help you make your dreams come true. You may find that the Divine has some changes in mind for you that can make life happier. You start to see your place in the Universe more clearly, and with that comes the ability to manifest abundance, romance, health, or whatever you're looking for.

In this book, I shed Divine Light on different divination tools, or oracles. Whatever you call them, they're all simply ways of talking to the Universe. Some will feel right to you, while others might not. My main purpose in writing *Compendium of Magical Things* is to take the fear and intimidation out of these languages of the Divine and (hopefully) give you a new way to get the answers and the guidance you seek. If you test out each of these methods, you may find that one of them works significantly better than the methods you are using or any you may have tried in the past. And wouldn't that be a wonderful thing?

The topics in this book are vast and complex, but I've tried to make them clear and easy to understand. That being said, if I were to cover every aspect of each of these topics, we'd have to rename this book *Encyclopedia of Magical Things*! Many books have been written on all of these topics, so if one or more of these methods of chatting up the Universe really appeals to you, I suggest you do further reading and study. But as you do so, keep in your heart the lack of fear and the unending love of the Divine that each method offers. If you're going to study further, choose resources that aren't fear based. As you try out these ancient tools, let your heart be your guide. A joyful heart is a sign that you're on the right track!

It is my fervent hope that you will go on this journey that I've loved so much. I've done everything I can to make it easy for you. I hope that you'll walk away with several oracles you like and spend some time in "Synchronicity City." But if you walk away with just one new way you like to commune with the Universe, that'll make me extremely happy!

Bon voyage!

CHAPTER 1

READ ME!

I'm very aware that this is the type of book where you might be tempted to just hop around from chapter to chapter all willy-nilly. And to an extent, you *could* do that. That being said, I placed each chapter in a specific order for a reason, and I rather think that reading this book in sequence will give you the broadest understanding of each Divine language touched upon in this compendium. If your personal, spiritual guidance leads you to read it in a different order, then of course I encourage you to do that.

However, it's especially important to read this chapter (and the introduction) before playing hop, skip, and jump within this book. This will give you a brief understanding of what to expect and some basic information on oracles that'll help tie everything together and make sure you don't become a lost ball in high weeds from the start. (Why, yes, I *was* born in the southern United States. How'd you know?) Chapter 1 also gives you some information about who I am and what my belief systems look like. So if this is our first meeting, then howdy-do! I'm very pleased to meet you.

Alrighty then. If you didn't read the introduction, go do it now. Go ahead! I'll wait for you here while you read it . . .

Okay—finished the introduction? Good! Onward we go!

First stop: the basics.

GOD IS BIG!

First, let's get this one thing settled. I consider God, Source, the Divine, the Universe, Goddess, the All That Is—all these words and more—to just be a bunch of different names for the same thing. So no matter which word I use in this book, know that to me they're all synonyms. If you have a word you like better than the one I used, then pretend I used that word. Just change it in your head as you read. Deal?

Okay. Now what was I saying? Oh, right! God is BIG! *I mean like, really, really big.*

The Universe is an amazing, awesomely powerful place where a million magical things can happen every minute. In fact, we could change that to a *bazillion* magical things every *second*, and we'd still be underestimating the power of the Divine.

So when someone says something like "God can perform miracles, but pendulums or oracle cards can't be real," that just makes me chuckle. When someone believes that God created the Earth in a certain number of days but doesn't believe that astrology has any viable effect on our lives, I just grin and quietly shake my head.

Have you ever noticed that human beings have a tendency to want to put God in a box? You know . . . a nice little place where what *they* believe is "all there is," and anything outside of that box isn't real. It's a very human thing to do. Quite understandable. But you have to remember that the Infinite is just that: *infinite.* Quite beyond our comprehension. When we refer to *Source*, we're just trying to put words and thoughts around something we can't fully understand so long as we're in these human bodies. Once we are no longer in the physical realm and have crossed over into spirit, things become very clear. But here's the scoop: God doesn't fit in a box. God doesn't fit in a building or even on the biggest planet you could fathom. Because God . . . is . . . BIG!

Source is perfectly capable of joyfully making any and all belief systems work simultaneously. The Divine relishes talking to you through tarot cards, runes, meditation, or just good old-fashioned prayer. There's no limit. There's only the language of the Divine that resonates the best for you. If runes aren't your thing, then leave them be. But cast aside the belief that because they don't work for *you,* they must not work for *anyone.* That's just putting God in a box.

By the way, even though some of these divination tools are referred to by practitioners as fortune-telling, that's a term that's never sat right with me. The term seems to indicate that something is fated or can't be changed. To me, this flies in the face of the concept of free will. We can *always* change where we're headed. That is one of our most magical gifts from the Divine.

THERE ARE SO MANY BEAUTIFUL PATHS

Why do you think there are so many and such varied spiritual paths? Why are there New Agers, Christians, Pagans, Muslims, Buddhists, Hindus, and people reaching out in a bazillion other ways to the Divine on planet Earth?

The reason is simple: we are all different. We are all magical, amazing, and unique children of God or Goddess or Source or the Universe . . . whatever name you want to give it. There is no one "right" way to find your path to the Divine because there is no one way to be human. No one way to exist. No one way to be.

Sure, it's possible that there is just one way for you in *this* lifetime. But it is incorrect to presume that just because there is one way for you this time around, it must therefore be the only way for everyone else. It may not even be the right way for you the next time around!

This dogged "my way or the highway" approach is where some religions get us into trouble. This is where some religions fail us.

We come to earth to grow. To learn. To evolve. To express our unique nature in unique ways. The lessons we seek to master are different with each incarnation. While in spirit, we tailor our next earthly experiences to give us the most evolution and joy! Think of it this way: you can take the same class over and over, but after a few times, you're not really gonna learn that much from taking that class again. The same concept is true of our spiritual paths.

Beyond that, we were given free will. At the time of this writing, there are 7.5 billion souls on this beautiful world. To give them all free will and then say "you must act in this one way" is basically giving a gift only to immediately demand that it be relinquished.

I have no right nor frankly any desire to judge your path. In my opinion, no one has that right. I have no idea what amazing, magical things you have planned for your current incarnation on this beautiful planet. I will admit that I'm quite curious! I love hearing your stories and your perceptions. But I do not judge your path because to do so openly invites you to judge mine.

And I'm not super into being judged. I'm betting you aren't either.

MY MAGICAL JOB

I consider myself a spiritual teacher. That's my job, and I *love* it! My life purpose, I've realized, is to give you spiritual things to think about without any fear. I want to open your mind to the notion that everything that *can* possibly exist *does* exist! Fear-based concepts in spirituality are human constructs that have virtually nothing to do with Source. More than anything, I want to set you free so that you can joyfully communicate with angels (more on them in Chapter 2), fairies (more on them in Chapter 3), and anything else that puts a smile on your face and a feeling of happiness in your heart.

One of the things I love so very much is when I teach something at a seminar or in front of a large crowd and then people tell me afterward that what I spoke about really made sense to them. The words that the Universe put in my mouth that day made a difference in their lives—wow! That makes me so happy.

If what I believe provides you with inspiration, gives you insights that feel "right" to you, eases your journey, or awakens your understanding of your own path toward joy, then I'd be deeply humbled. Gosh darn it, I'd be downright overjoyed! I would also be equally as humbled to have been of service if what

I teach doesn't quite resonate with you but in some way still awakens you to what would work on your journey.

You see, many spiritual teachers have brought me great inspiration. What they have taught, I keep close to my heart. But here's the thing. (And this is important. I really want you to get this.) Any given teacher may have helped me understand what it means to be a spiritual being while having a human experience; in the end, however, the understanding happened within *me*. Likewise, if what I teach leads you to an awakening, then the credit for that goes to *you*. A teacher helped you find your path, but the finding of the path was your brilliant work, not mine—or anyone else's.

One of the things I want to caution you about as you start this part of your journey is something I call the comparison trap. This is when we compare ourselves—our accomplishments, beliefs, or spiritual paths—to others. When we make such comparisons, we almost always find ourselves lacking. In trying to judge our own successes as compared to others', we stop following our own life purpose and begin trying to mirror someone else's. This rarely turns out well, and I *highly* recommend you don't do that. Yes, be curious! Yes, learn, respect, and support. But in the end, your path is perfect for you, and it matters not one iota that your path is different from the paths of the people you learn from.

NO PEDESTALS, PLEASE

People sometimes place spiritual teachers on a pedestal. We put God in a box and human spiritual teachers on a pedestal. Isn't that crazy? Nevertheless, I see this happen all the time. The problem with this is that it gives your power away to another person.

When I travel and meet people before or after events or in book-signing lines, I hug *everyone*. I look them in the eye and ask their name and laugh with them. The reason I do this is that I don't want them to put me on a pedestal. What I want is for others to see me as *Radleigh*—as someone who's approachable and won't judge their path or have an agenda about their beliefs. Going along with my desire to be open and approachable, I communicate with my students every single day on social media. My Certified Angel Tarot Reader and Certified Angel Card Reader students talk about serious issues, but we also joke back and forth with one another all the time. And I love them!

Another problem with pedestals is people can fall off them. If you've placed your faith in a particular person as the source for all your answers and spiritual guidance, then you may find yourself feeling lost, confused, or even devastated if they can't live up to the expectations you've placed upon them. And the truth is people are human. They make mistakes. They change.

Here's how I see things: If you find that walking along with me on this spiritual path brings you guidance and epiphanies, then that's wonderful! Let's walk together! You can learn what the angels have shared with me, and I'll learn what Source has shared with you, and both of us will hold each other up with love.

And both of us will be fully empowered with our own magical piece of God in our hearts where it belongs.

THE TEACHER IS NOT THE TEACHINGS

Please also remember that the teacher is not the teachings. When I write or speak in front of crowds, the Divine wisdom that comes forth is often as much a surprise to me as it is to anyone listening. Often, I'm learning as I'm teaching, because Spirit and the angels just speak through me. I learned a long time ago that trying to write out or plan what I'm teaching onstage isn't just a waste of time, but it's actually detrimental to the message. I might have an outline just to make sure I don't miss an important point, but that's it. To me, trusting what comes through feels like putting my metaphorical Rad-car in neutral and letting it go where Source wants it to go. I'm aware that I'm talking, and I'm experiencing the thought and the next thought and the thought after that queuing up in my head, but it's only partly me.

I love to make people laugh. I feel that the best way for people to experience their own revelations is poignancy through laughter. So the jokes? Those are me. The epiphanies? Those come from the angels and the Divine.

Do you see what I'm saying here? That's why I say the teacher and the teachings are not the same thing. I say that because if at some later date I were to "fall off a pedestal," you can know in your heart that the things we learned together in my writings or in my teachings are still valid. They're still real. The joy and the blessings have always come from the Universe. Radleigh was just a (hopefully) funny and always sparkly spokesperson for the Divine. (Why sparkly? Well, I wear a lot of sequins.)

Nothing can take your beliefs away from you, so long as you don't put me or anyone else on a pedestal. Keep your power!

And for what it's worth, I'm afraid of heights.

YOU'RE A MAGICAL DROP OF WATER

Life is magic. I say that all the time. But what does that even mean? Where does the magic come from? And what makes divination tools work anyway?

You can think of it this way: Imagine a big fountain. Make it one of those really big ones you see in Europe or at public buildings, the kind that people in romantic comedies dance around in. The water in that fountain is the Divine. Now, imagine that the fountain turns on and water sprays into the air. Those little drops of water? They're us: you, me, everyone you ever knew, and everyone who ever lived.

That's right. We're all magical little manifesting pieces of the Universe. While we're on the wild ride of being forced up into the air with all the others who are currently having a physical existence, we can forget our Source, where we came from. God is that huge pool of water beneath us, and we'll eventually return to that pool, because there's nowhere else for us to go. But while we're "separated," we forget just how magical life is. We forget that as tiny, miraculous drops of the Divine, we have that same Divine magic within us to create a heavenly experience—or we can create the opposite.

On that note, the "opposite" is just a miserable, unmagical experience. Just so you know, I don't believe in hell. Hell is simply a human construct to make God small and petty and to control people. The only hell that exists is the one that we create for ourselves during any given lifetime.

Here's another analogy. (Be warned: I *love* analogies.) Imagine that the little spark of the Divine within you is a small battery—maybe a button cell battery, or a AAA battery, or whatever small size is available in your country. This battery isn't very big or powerful. But imagine if the billions of little batteries on earth now were put together with every person's battery who'd ever lived on earth. Imagine how much energy that would be— it would be enormous!

At any given moment, the reality you're experiencing is a combination of what your little battery is giving energy to and what we as a world are focusing on together with our batteries. To take the metaphor one step further, if you put your battery in a toy car, then there's energy given to the car. The car is reality to you. But if you take the battery out of the car and place it instead in a mechanical talking animal, then the energy is now fueling something new. The car without batteries will not move, and it will fade from your attention and eventually be forgotten. Your reality has shifted to where you have devoted your energy.

Most of our batteries in the world are focused on the sky being blue and the grass being green and whatever big news story is currently scrolling in our social media feeds or on our televisions. And so we make it real.

That's how the Universe works. And this is also what fuels divination tools. Over the centuries, people have focused their energy on these ways to communicate with God. They've believed in them. And in doing so, they gave them true life. The energy they gave is still there. So when you lend your energy and attention to them, you're actually connecting with those same energetic lines to Source.

SO . . . WHO ARE WE TALKING TO EXACTLY?

When you do divinatory work, the messages you receive are coming to you from various sources. Each time you interpret such messages, that process is called a reading. As you learn from this compendium about all the different ways to do readings, you might choose to learn to do them for yourself. Or you might decide you love the idea of the readings, but you'd like to consult a professional. Personally, I do both. I read for myself via tarot and angel work, but I go to professionals when it comes to astrology, even though I do know a lot about it. It's all about personal preference and whatever you're comfortable with.

The reading itself comes from, first and foremost, your connection with the Divine. That little bit of Source energy that is within you is eternally connected to the "all that is" of the Universe. This connection is made of Light; it's like an invisible fiber-optic cable. If you choose to work with guardian angels or archangels, then the information you receive may come from them as emissaries of God. (We'll talk more about that in Chapter 2.)

Another place that the information may come from is your subconscious. Sometimes the Divine may answer your prayers or requests for information by triggering your subconscious to give up one of its many mysteries. It comes as an aha moment, when suddenly you're awake to your own actions or motives. This kind of moment often feels like your own revelation—and it might be. But if it comes while working with an oracle or a divination tool, it more likely came from your connection to God and the seeking you were doing at the time.

Keep in mind that talking to the Divine is good for you! It clears your energy, and you'll feel better and more confident.

Life will seem easier and more joyful. You'll become more optimistic.

EGO—UH-OH!

Within all of us, there's an annoying little voice called the ego. It's the voice that tells you that you "can't do this" or you're "not smart enough to do that." It's also the primary thing that gets in the way of doing divinatory or revelatory work with oracles. It's the nagging little voice that'll tell you tarot cards are dumb and astrology couldn't possibly work. Even if it does allow for these things to be real, it'll assure you that you have no such Divine gifts to allow you to be able to get information from any oracle.

Messages that you receive from any divinatory tool that are mean-spirited, unkind, or in any way not empowering or uplifting aren't coming from the Divine. They're coming from your ego.

That isn't to say that a heads-up of impending challenges is false. It may be true! I always appreciate information I receive that allows me to take action to avoid undesirable outcomes. However, true messages from Source that provide opportunities to avoid unwanted outcomes will always be delivered with kindness and compassion. It won't be a message of "Everything is ruined!" Instead, it might be a message that says, "You're headed somewhere you don't want to go, so you might want to make changes." Or you might hear, "We know things are unhappy right now, but here's the way out!"

SYNCHRONICITY CITY

I live in a magical (and metaphorical) placed called Synchronicity City. You won't find Synchronicity City on any maps—at least, no map I know of. (Maybe I should Google that.) Synchronicities are a big way that the Universe talks to us. Some people mistake them for coincidences, but time and experience have dispelled the myth of coincidences for me.

When magical things happen in parallel to one another, that's a sign from the Divine. Seeing particular sequences of numbers or seeing the same number repetitively are common signs. The number 444 is largely associated with the message "Angels are with you." So if you wake up at 4:44 A.M. and your latte costs $4.44 and the license plate on the car in front of you ends in 444, and then you get out of your car at work and step over a white feather (another sign of angels) lying on the ground, that's not coincidence. That's synchronicity. That's Source (and the angels) trying to get your attention.

Many oracles use synchronicities to validate their messages. So you're sure to be visiting Synchronicity City as you work through this compendium.

In fact, while writing this book, I was amazed to see the *exact* same messages show up as I worked with different divination tools, which validated the accuracy of each of the methods! In cross-referencing messages from the oracles, incredible clarity and epiphanies were given to me. I never stopped being completely awestruck when each oracle would back up the other.

As I moved from one oracle to another, I would call a dear friend of mine even more than usual to share all the exciting news. I would become so excited every time an oracle would perfectly explain a situation I was asking about. Or when the Runes would validate what the I Ching said. Or when tarot and the Lenormand would practically hold hands and sing the same song to me. I thought, *It's almost like all of these oracles are connected.*

And that's when it hit me: Of course they're connected! They're all just lines of communication reaching out to Source and back again.

I've been living in Synchronicity City for months now, and let me tell you, it's an awesome place. I love it here!

TO BE PERFECTLY CLAIR

There are four primary ways people tend to receive information through oracle work. These ways are the "clairs," which always makes me think of Aunt Clara on the TV show *Bewitched*. I just loved her! (I bring up Aunt Clara only in the hopes that the connection might also help you remember the term *clairs*.)

The most commonly known clair is clairvoyance. People tend to use that word as a general term for psychic gifts, but that's a bit like using the brand name Kleenex to refer to all tissues or Coke to refer to all soft drinks. It's not correct, but it's very common. *Clairvoyance* actually refers to receiving psychic information in a visual way. This usually involves getting Divine messages through mental images in the "mind's eye." This is also how most people "see" angels and fairies. Clairvoyance is often highly desired in the intuitive community, but I believe all the clairs to be a blessing and equally as beautiful.

It's possible, but exceedingly rare, for someone's clairvoyance to manifest as seeing an image through their physical eyes in a psychic reading. After 30 years of studying this type of work, I've only known two people who said they literally saw things. Frankly, it's not something I would ever want for myself; it'd probably scare the bejeezus out of me or make me certain I was losing my mind!

The next clair is clairsentience. This is when psychic or intuitive information comes from someone's emotions or through physical feelings. A clairsentient person will feel the presence of angels or feel wary if someone is lying to them. They may feel sad for no reason they can put their finger on because someone near them is feeling sad. They might experience a tightness in their chest when in the presence of someone who has a heart condition. People with this clair should especially be careful to remove energetic attachments to other people and keep themselves shielded. (I'll talk more about the topic later in this chapter.)

Clairaudience works very much like clairvoyance. People with this gift hear things inside their mind rather than out loud as one might listen to music or hear a loved one ask a question. This isn't the same as "voices in their head," which would indicate an emotional challenge; this is the ability to tune in to messages from the Divine or the angels in an auditory way. This is one of my abilities, but as I usually receive Divine information through another channel, this is what I would refer to as a "secondary clair." My angels have sometimes communicated to me through this gift so that it actually does sound like someone has spoken to me out loud, but only in times of great importance and when I wasn't really listening in a spiritual way.

Finally, there's claircognizance. *Cognizance* is a sense of knowingness. This is my primary clair and also the rarest form of clair. It's when you just *know* something, like who's calling on the phone or that someone isn't being truthful. It can be the trickiest of the clairs to navigate as it takes time and practice to learn the difference between your thoughts, your ego, and Divine communication.

There are additional clairs that involve things like smell (clairalience), taste (clairgustance), and touch (clairtangency), but they're extremely rare.

ENERGETIC CONNECTIONS: ALL TIED UP

Two skills imperative to intuitive work are shielding yourself from and severing unwanted energetic connections. Frankly, I think of these two practices as just basic stuff I need to do each day whether I'm engaged in intuitive work or not. It's sort of like brushing my teeth or combing my hair.

Energetic connections (sometimes called energy strands or cords) are the connections we make on a daily basis to people, things, and even beliefs. Imagine these cords now, linking you to things around you. Usually, the longer they've been around, the larger they are, so imagine them as ranging in size from fine fishing line all the way up to thick fire hose. These connections form naturally whenever you have an interaction with anyone. You can also form energy connections to inanimate objects because energy runs through everything on the planet. These connections can drain your energy, adversely affect your health, and just generally bring you down. That's why it's so important to keep them cleared away. Fortunately, this is relatively simple to do.

Because I work so closely with angels, my usual method is to ask Archangel Michael to clear away all energetic connections that aren't serving me or are draining my personal energy. I envision him using his sword of Light in front of me, behind me, on either side, and above and below me—clearing away all energy connections except those that are to the Divine. Because these connections occur constantly, it's a good idea to ask Archangel Michael to clear them away daily. Consider adding this to your routine when you get up or before you go to bed.

There are many other great ways to clear away energetic connections. I highly recommend picking up *Energy Strands* by the amazing Denise Linn; it's the best book I've ever read on the topic.

Once you have removed unwanted energetic connections, you're going to want to shield yourself from acquiring new ones! When it comes to shielding, I once again turn to Archangel Michael, the amazing angel of protection who resonates to a deep royal blue color. Ask him to place a shielding bubble of that blue around you every morning. This will keep other people from forming an energetic connection to you as you go through your day. On particularly challenging days, I'll ask Archangel Michael to place a titanium steel ball of energy around me! Of course, you can also ask for the same sort of protection from Source, God, or whoever you reach out to for Divine protection. And that's all you need to do—ask.

PREPARING TO WORK WITH YOUR ORACLES

There are seven important things to do to set yourself up for success when it comes to doing an oracle reading.

1. Oracles that you hold in your hand—such as tarot and oracle cards, pendulums, and runes—require clearing and consecration before you work with them.

There are many effective clearing methods. One of the most common is to envision white light coming down from heaven, through the top of your head (your crown chakra), down into your dominant hand, and then letting that white light leave your hand and fill up the oracle.

Other methods are to leave the tools in the moonlight for a night (weather permitting) or to smudge them. To smudge something, you burn a bundle of sage (known as a smudge stick), and allow the smoke to surround all sides of the object. Some items can be placed briefly in salt and then washed off, so long as the material it is made of won't be damaged by the salt. For example, some pendulums and runes are made of delicate crystal, so you might want to choose methods other than salt for clearing.

As for consecrating or blessing your divination tools, a simple prayer to whatever higher power you resonate with will suffice. I recommend a prayer that is heartfelt and indicates your desire to commune with the Divine in a way that brings you closer to your own life purpose and be of service to others. As an example, here is a prayer I use to bless and consecrate my cards:

> *Mother, Father, God. Thank you for love and thank you for Light. Thank you for magic, and wonderment, and awakening, and knowing, and believing, and seeing. I ask that you bless these cards. I ask that the readings I do with them be of value and of service. I ask that the messages that they bring to me and to others be crystal clear and easy to understand, leading to healing, to transformation, and to happiness. And so it is.*

Of course, you can create whatever type of prayer feels right to you and gives you a sense that you are connected with the oracle through Divine Light.

2. Know that other people's energy can affect your readings, so you'll need to clear and consecrate your oracles regularly.

Whether you're doing readings for yourself or someone else, there are other things you need to keep in mind. First of all, there's no consensus on whether you should let other people handle or touch your oracles. Some say absolutely not! Others say it doesn't matter or even that it helps with the reading. (I'm in the "absolutely not" club.)

Whatever you believe, if you do let others touch your divination tool, which is more common with cards and runes, you'll need to clear them before doing a reading for someone else. Otherwise, the energy of the person who last touched them can show up in the next reading and really confuse everyone!

Even if you haven't let someone physically touch your oracles, others' energy might seem to linger. If your readings seem to become muddled or difficult to decipher, then clear and consecrate your tools again in order to bring them back into full alignment with your personal energy.

3. Pray or meditate with an oracle before each use.

I use the following prayer before doing readings. If you like it, feel free to use it! Or you can create your own prayer or meditation to use before your readings.

Archangels Uriel, Haniel, Jeremiel, and Raziel, I ask that you be with me for any readings that I do today. Let these readings be of value, be of purpose, be of meaning. Let them really make a difference in people's lives; let them be of service. Let me see, hear, feel, and know the words of Spirit so as to convey the words of Spirit in such a way as to enlighten, to inspire, and to heal. I ask that Archangel Gabriel give me the perfect words for these readings so that their meaning will be clear to the recipient. And so it is.

4. Do your readings in a peaceful, quiet place.

Choose a calm place to do your readings—preferably somewhere that is set aside specifically for prayer, meditation, and oracle work. You might want to light a candle or some incense. Do whatever makes you feel at peace.

5. Keep your feet and legs uncrossed.

Another thing to keep in mind is that it's best to do readings with your feet and legs uncrossed. I prefer to have my feet firmly on the ground so that I'm completely—well—grounded! Crossing your legs or feet blocks off the energy from you to the other in a reading—or even from yourself and Source. While it doesn't completely cut you off, it definitely muffles the messages.

6. Be mindful of the wording of your questions.

The Universe is literal. How you phrase a question is very important when working with an oracle. Many oracles don't handle "or" questions very well. Asking your oracle "Should I buy the blue car or the red car?" will more often than not get you an answer that doesn't make sense. Instead, ask the oracle, "Should I buy the blue car?" and wait for your answer. Then ask, "Should I buy the red car?" and wait for the next answer. If you get a favorable answer to both cars, then you can't lose! If you get a negative answer to both cars, then keep shopping.

Really think about a question before you ask it. If someone asked you the same question, would you find aspects of it confusing or incomplete? Could the question be interpreted to mean multiple things? Be specific. Be crystal clear.

7. Be in a calm and peaceful state before doing a reading.

Trying to get answers from oracles when you're emotionally charged can be a challenge. When people are upset while doing a reading, their egos can take over. A card in tarot that means "wish come true" can seem like certain doom if you're in fear.

Of course, when our emotions are running high is often the very moment we want our oracles' help! If you can't reach a state of calm, ask a friend or a professional for the answers you seek.

Over time, you'll be able to set aside your emotions and ask your own questions. You'll learn how not to see the worst in the message. Be patient with yourself.

R-E-S-P-E-C-T!

Your oracles aren't toys. They should always be treated with respect if you want *them* to take *you* seriously. So don't ask your oracles silly questions unless you're just starting out and need to test if you have things right. For example, you might ask your pendulum "Am I female?" as a way to discover which direction it swings for a yes or no answer.

Be in a spirit of humility when asking a question. (After all, you *are* talking to God.) Always show gratitude after your session with the oracle is over. And make sure you keep your divination tools stored in a peaceful place where they won't be disturbed by others.

Be fully present when consulting your oracles. If you're asking a question about whether to take that new job offer, for example, but then your mind drifts to what's for dinner as you shuffle your tarot cards, you're bound to get gibberish for an answer.

Oracles will often answer the question that is most pressing on your heart even if you ask something else. If your career question gets you an answer that sounds for all the world like a romance reading, then pause and ask yourself "Is this just as important as the question I asked?" Allow the reading to play out; then ask your career question again. Once you have an answer to the question within your subconscious, your oracle will usually then return to your original question.

Also on the topic of respect, many oracle practitioners refer to their practice as a science. In particular, astrologers, numerologists, dowsers, and the practitioners of mantra consider their areas of study to be science. In this compendium, I have chosen to respect their description of what they practice without debating semantics. There's an awful lot out there in the Universe we don't understand, so who's to say if they're right or wrong?

Certainly not I.

HISTORY AND MYTHS

Most of the oracles explored in this book have long and complex histories, and some have powerful myths associated with them as well. It simply isn't possible to include all of that information in this compendium without making it 5,000 pages long—or even longer! So at the beginning of each chapter, I've included a *short* summary of the history of these oracles for you. If a particular oracle really calls to you, then you might want to understand its origins in depth by researching online or seeking out some books.

I do think that history and myths matter. I think it's power-ful to know where your Divine language came from. However, I don't think those things matter very much when you're just trying to discover which oracle you want to pursue. You can test out working with a pendulum without knowing its background. But if the pendulum delights you, then why wouldn't you want to learn about your new friend's history?

THE LAW OF ATTRACTION

The Law of Attraction comes up in various forms throughout this compendium. The basic tenet is that what you place your focus on is what you bring into your reality. If you focus on the positive things you want, then that is what you'll manifest. If, like most people, you focus instead on negative things that are happening in your life or on the absence of what you're desiring, then you'll simply manifest more of the negative or the absence.

In order to manifest a magical life, I truly, truly believe that we must stay in control of our thoughts. However, that being said, I do know that when things seem bleak with no end in sight, it can be hard to be positive about your life.

Let's say that you're feeling like you don't have enough money. That's the "reality" you're experiencing. You feel broke, so you focus on your *lack* of money. What this creates in your life via the Law of Attraction is more lack of money. In order to correct this, you need to change your thoughts and your focus, perhaps by focusing on the things that you *do* have that are wonderful. You might then take an action step toward increasing your abundance, meditate to clear your mind, or use one of the oracles in this book to help you manifest more prosperity.

Let me give you a real example from my own life of how the Law of Attraction can affect your reality.

In the summer of 2017, I was under a tremendous amount of stress. Good stress, mind you! Wonderful things happening! Just too many things at once. Too many deadlines. Lots of high expectations upon me from people I respect and care about and didn't want to let down. On top of that, the summer is always my heaviest travel season.

And so I caught a cold. Great. I went through three boxes of tissues in four days. Seriously, I really did.

Of course, that was just the Divine forcing me to take a break. And while I heeded that, I still needed to pull myself together and go to the pharmacy for supplies. While I was in there, I noticed one of those little blood pressure machines. I'd never used one, but I was curious. So I sat down, and (shocker) my blood pressure was high. Not sky high, mind you, but high. I tried it again. Same result.

I went home to rest, but now I was worried. I was obsessing about the issue of my health. It was the weekend, so there was no way to see my doctor. I decided to go to another pharmacy to test myself on another machine and, sure enough, got the same results. So the next day, I went to another pharmacy. Same results. (Please understand that I am not a hypochondriac, nor have I ever been. But I was totally obsessing about this issue.)

I finally got to see my doctor about this on Monday. He tested me, and my blood pressure was still high. But he talked to me about my life and my health, asking very pointed questions. He assured me I was not sick, but he would do tests.

The results of the test were golden. I couldn't be healthier. So he tested my blood pressure again, and it had dropped 10 points. He then forbade me to ever, *ever* use one of those blood pressure machines again.

Smart doctor, right? He knew that I had created my own problem.

When our thoughts go negative and stay there, we create our own problems. Or at the very least, we make them worse. Worry and regret and fear don't help. Fretting about the problem and worrying is just like me and my blood pressure. As I focused on it, it stayed a problem. When I let it go, it went away. If you don't focus on your unhappiness, you at least give it a chance to go away. So here are some sparks you can use to fuel the fires of positive thinking when things are tough:

- First, remind yourself that whatever is challenging you right now, you've got it. You can handle this. You really can. Give yourself credit for being stronger than you realize, and be determined not to let yourself become overwhelmed with your situation.

- Take action. If you have a challenge that needs attending to, think of one step you can take toward your goal, even if it's just a small step.

- If it's not a challenge that requires action, then take action anyway to make yourself feel better. For example, you can indulge small joys like eating your favorite dessert or going to a happy movie with a bubbly friend. But do something.

- Try something new, perhaps something you've always wanted to do or learn but always had a reason for putting off. Add a new positive experience or guilty pleasure to your life to uplift your mood.

- Remember to reflect on the things in your life that are good! There is always something worth being grateful for in your life. Turn your attention to those things. Keep a gratitude journal or make a list of things you're thankful for.

- Remove as many negative people from your life as you can. There will be some people—like family members—that you might feel you cannot remove, so remove as many others as you can. Doing so will give you added strength to deal with the "negative Nellies" in your life who you have to keep. It will also make room in your life for positive and supportive people to come in. Ask Archangel Raguel, the friend of God, to help you with that.

- Pretend you're happy. I'm serious. Fake it. Simply pretending that you're happy can lift your spirits and allow the focus on what's wrong to redirect to what's right. Think of what you usually do when you're happy, or think of the mannerisms of a happy person, and do one of those today. For example, sing along to the radio, skip, or smile when you don't really feel like it.

- Finally, remember that everything—*everything*—is temporary. The challenges you're facing will pass. The only way they won't is if you continue to obsess about them. So let them go. Remember the first thing I said? You've got this. You will prevail. I have faith in you.

All of this isn't as unscientific as you might first think. More and more, quantum physics is bridging the gap of spiritual concepts to show that placing our attention on the tiniest of elements in our universe changes their form!

If you're interested in learning about more ways of working with the Law of Attraction to make your dreams come true, I recommend picking up my book *How to Be Your Own Genie: Manifesting the Magical Life You Were Born to Live.*

SPREADING THE MAGIC AROUND

Many divination tools use a concept called spreads. Spreads are a specific pattern to lay down tarot cards, runes, and other oracles that use positions to provide specific parts of the reading. Some spreads are very simple, while others can be very complex. There are an endless selection of them for each tool in books and on the Internet.

For example, here's a very simple three-card spread you might use in a tarot- or oracle-card reading. After clearing, consecrating, and shuffling the cards, you'd ask your question; then lay the cards on a flat surface from left to right:

- **Card 1, the past:** This card tells you information that led to the situation you're asking about in your reading.

- **Card 2, the present:** This card tells you information about where things stand right now.

- **Card 3, the future:** This card tells you about the most likely outcome if no changes in action are taken.

WHAT TO DO AFTER A READING

A great way to learn an oracle is to use it daily—preferably in the morning. You can pull a card for the day or choose a rune. Then, as the day progresses, you can contemplate how that oracle's message relates to your experiences. Keeping a journal of these daily readings is also a powerful learning tool.

Both giving and receiving a reading is usually uplifting, enlightening, and magical. However, on occasion, you might get messages that you perceive to be distressing or worrisome. You might be getting a reading from someone who is inexperienced or just has a fear-based take on things. Or perhaps you're doing a reading for yourself about something that you were already feeling fear about. Sometimes the answer simply wasn't at all what you were expecting. How you react to that situation will probably reflect where you are spiritually and emotionally.

Here are some steps you might take to work through the worry and get a clearer understanding of the messages.

You can call upon Archangel Michael to calm your fears and worries, whether they're related to messages from the Divine or *anything* that has you concerned. In this situation, you would ask Archangel Michael to sever your energetic connections to fear, worry, and situations from the past that are causing your feelings. Also call upon the Archangel Uriel, who has the ability to offer you emotional healing as well as understanding of the message so that you truly comprehend what you are being told and can find balance. (I'll teach you lots more about how to work with angels in Chapter 2.)

Once you have these two amazing archangels near you, think about the reading. What was it that upset you? If the reading came from someone else, what was their demeanor? Was the message a fearful one or delivered in a harsh way? Are you upset that the reading didn't give you the answer you wanted? Be really honest with yourself; what you do next depends on the answers to those questions.

If what upset you was the demeanor of the reader or a message that was fear based in nature or delivered harshly, then shake it off. It's not you, it's the reader. There are bad apples in every career group, including spiritually based businesses. I know you'd think that wouldn't be the case, but it is. The best thing I can suggest is to get a reading from someone you can trust. Perhaps someone professionally trained like one of the thousands of Certified Angel Tarot Readers or Certified Angel Card Readers, who I've taught to read in a positive and uplifting way. You'll get reliable answers delivered with love and compassion from my students.

If what upset you was that you didn't get the answer you wanted, then the problem may lie within you. Was the direction or "likely outcome" of the reading *really* that bad or just not what you had dreamed up? Are you being rigid? Are you trying to tell the Universe how to do its job? Its "job," by the way, is to lead you toward your greatest happiness. It often knows something you don't know about the best way to get there.

If the message wasn't that bad—just different from your expectations—then I'd recommend spending some time contemplating that. Maybe this is a path to happiness you hadn't considered. Maybe it's just step one to getting where you want to go. Readings like this can also be a heads-up that you need a course correction. If that's the case, maybe you should be grateful for this information rather than letting it worry you.

And most of all, always, always remember that you have free will! Any reading is always just the most likely scenario at any given moment *if* you continue to move along as you are now. You can change your actions, plans, or direction at any time and change the likely outcome of your path. Anyone who tells you differently is someone you should avoid seeing ever again at all costs.

Okay, I think that about covers the basics. Now you're ready to talk to the Universe!

CHAPTER 2

THE MAGIC OF ANGELS

IS WORKING WITH ANGELS THE RIGHT CHOICE FOR YOU?

- Do you often have the feeling that you're being watched over?

- Do you come across white feathers, lucky pennies, or other objects that have special meaning to you in moments of need?

- Do you sometimes see movement out of the corner of your eye, and when you turn, there's nothing there?

- Does the idea of angels make you feel safe, comforted, or happy?

When it comes to spirituality, angels have always been my first love. There's no doubt in my heart or mind that angels are real. I've experienced their touch in my life over and over. My earliest communication with an angel that I can remember was at age five. That's when my primary guardian angel, Joshua, woke me from a deep sleep to warn me that the house across the street was on fire.

I've also encountered thousands upon thousands of other people in my travels who've had the same experience. In fact, most children's "imaginary friends" are actually guardian angels. These kids just haven't been talked out of seeing them yet.

That's why, from my standpoint, the answer to the question "Is working with angels the right choice for you?" is a resounding *yes!* Yes for everyone! Because you have angels! And *you* have angels! And *you* have angels! Angels for *everyone!*

Sorry. I had a little Oprah moment there, but I'm back now.

Really, though, I don't know why anyone wouldn't want to work with angels. Yet I do know that some consider angels to be too "fluffy" or "too attached to religion." Neither of those things are really the case—let's see if I can win you over.

Angels are often thought of as messengers, like the grand "postal service" of the Divine. However, they do far more than just deliver heavenly mail. Angels are pure love—an endless source of unconditional support and Divine energy. Prayers to these great winged ones have brought about miracles in my life and the lives of countless others. I'm no longer surprised when magical things happen in my life and I then receive a message from the angels that they are with me. I'm no longer surprised, but I continue to be endlessly grateful when something my ego tells me I don't deserve but that I desperately want is dropped into my lap by my angels. Stories abound of people who were helped by a stranger who was just suddenly there at the time of their need and then gone as soon as help had been provided.

Angels are also omnipresent—able to be everywhere at once. You should never worry about asking the angels for assistance. The angels *want* to help! You're not keeping them from more "important" tasks; they're of the Divine and therefore can be anywhere and everywhere at the same time. You can ask them for assistance in anything from the failing health of a loved one to the need for extra money or an excellent grade on a test.

JUST A *LITTLE* HISTORY

It's true that a lot of what we "know" about angels comes from religious texts. Many people think that they're largely a Judeo-Christian-based belief, but belief in angels is far broader than that. The truth is that stories of their place in human lives weaves through the history of all humankind.

While the major religions of the world may fuss and feud about a whole bunch of topics, they generally seem to agree that angels exist. Some of the religions that talk about angels include Buddhism, Christianity, Hinduism, Islam, Judaism, and Mormonism. However, these prominent religions that mention these beings of light and love do not all call such beings by the same name. *Devas, apsaras, malaikah,* and *ministering spirits* are some of the other terms used to describe these entities with a common set of characteristics. Also interesting to note is that some of the most common names for archangels (Gabriel, Michael, Raphael, and Uriel) cross religious lines in varying forms.

Some ancient texts refer to wrathful angels and fallen angels. These texts also always portray God as quite angry, punishing, and unforgiving. To me, that makes God small and petty and not BIG and loving. For that reason, I do not believe in fallen angels. It makes no sense to me that the messengers and helpers of the Divine would just run amok. That'd mean they have egos. But angels don't have egos. I also don't believe in wrathful angels because what would their purpose be?

THE DIFFERENT TYPES OF ANGELS

There are many kinds of angels. Levels and tiers of these helpers of mankind sent by God are outlined in ancient texts. There are three types that are the most called upon: guardian angels, archangels, and "special purpose" angels.

Guardian Angels: The information that's been provided to me via angels, the Divine, and countless conversations with other "angelfolk" (fans of angels and people who work with angels) is that *everyone* is born with at least two guardian angels watching over them. (Some people have many more.) These guardian angels follow us from lifetime to lifetime; thus, they know us far better than we know ourselves. They're quite aware of everything we're here on earth to accomplish, even though we're rarely conscious of that information ourselves.

Archangels: Archangels are very different from guardian angels. They're here for all people, not just a particular person.

While there are countless archangels, 15 are the most well known: Ariel, Azrael, Chamuel, Gabriel, Haniel, Jeremiel, Jophiel, Metatron, Michael, Raguel, Raphael, Raziel, Sandalphon, Uriel, and Zadkiel. The *el* at the end of most of their names means "of God," and archangels are considered to be angels of high "rank" who often supervise or watch over more common angels.

There can be all kinds of variant spelling of their names, which makes researching them a challenge. Also, sometimes one ancient text gives an archangel credit for doing something while another text gives the credit to a different archangel.

Each of the archangels have their own specialties and traits. For example, Archangel Michael is known for protection and safety, helping people with their life purpose, and dissolving away connections to people or things that aren't good for them. Archangels also tend to radiate to particular colors. Continuing our example, Archangel Michael appears in a deep royal blue or purple color.

For more information on these amazing archangels and their specialties, check out my book *How to Be Your Own Genie*. I've outlined the whole scoop in Chapter 5 of that book.

Special Purpose Angels: Finally, there are what I call special purpose angels. Sometimes in my work, I'll discover that someone has an additional angel hanging out with them that isn't a guardian angel. For example, perhaps a person is struggling with a health challenge and has asked the Divine for help with that. A special purpose angel may come to assist until the health challenge has passed and then move on to someone else who is need of extra angelic support. Angelfolk often call upon romance angels for help in relationships and prosperity angels for help with financial or material needs, or even just to get help with a parking space in a very crowded city!

No, really. I do that last thing. In case you're wondering, the parking space angel's name is Walter.

WHY WORKING WITH THE GREAT WINGED ONES IS SO EASY

There are several reasons why connecting with angels might work well for someone searching for a belief system. For starters, angels are a great connection for those that are extremely sensitive or new to spiritual exploration. Sensitive souls may find some of the imagery in tarot to be frightening (though certainly not in the decks I've created), or they may experience the puzzle-like work of astrology to be too complicated and a little cold with its focus on math. The experience of angels, however, can be quite palpable and moving and is always comforting.

For those who experienced conservative religious upbringings, or even those who were raised in very scientific households, pursuing spiritual paths can fill us with fear of reprisals from both God and peers alike. Angels, however, can be a way to start to expand one's spiritual horizons that feels safe from possible negative feedback from people who don't understand. Angels feel very comfortable and aren't controversial to most people with strong religious beliefs. For example, believing in angels isn't going to upset your Catholic Aunt Edna one tiny bit.

Angels also require very little study or academic pursuit. In fact, a belief in angels as protectors and beings of light is often instilled in us from a very early age. Once you understand the basics of communication and perhaps the differences between the 15 major archangels, you pretty much have all you need to fully immerse yourself. When compared with more complex methodologies—the I Ching, astrology, numerology, etc.— angels are very simple to work with and are easily accessible.

You can talk to them anywhere! Whether it's in your car, your home, or your office, they're always available to you. I'm always astonished at the number of people who say they talk to their angels in the shower!

HOW YOU RECEIVE MESSAGES FROM YOUR ANGELS

Angels are direct messengers from the Divine—pure and simple. They're quite literally designed to communicate with us if we just ask for their help and then make the effort to receive their messages.

If and when you start to work with angels, your primary guardian angel will likely be the first to introduce themselves. Other angels may also show up right away, or they might wait months or even years to present themselves. If they do take a while to appear, it could be that it's in your best interest to focus your attention on just one angel for now. However, others may still be standing by and actively assisting you behind the scenes.

As I mentioned in Chapter 1, people can connect with their intuitive abilities in several different ways, called the clairs. Angels lend themselves to whichever clair, or sense, a person may feel most connected with. Whether it's sight, sound, thought, or feeling, angels are going to work with you in the way you feel most comfortable.

It's important to understand that angels come from a place of love and support and tend to speak in such a way that you can clearly hear their messages. This can be a different experience for each person.

For example, when I was growing up, the world was a very unsafe place. I was very alone and almost constantly in a state of fear. What I wanted more than anything in the world was an older brother. Someone who'd love and protect me. It therefore makes perfect sense that, even to this day, Joshua speaks to me in just that way! Because I'm always laughing, Joshua tends to make jokes, tease me, and even lovingly make fun of me.

Actually, it's his sense of humor that's so appealing to me. I'm still able to understand the real message he's sending me and make the most use of it. If he were very serious and proper, that just wouldn't be me.

I'm perfectly aware that a teasing "older brother" might be the worst thing ever for some people. It would be very difficult for some people to get a message if it were wrapped up in a joke. Have no fear. Guardian angels tailor their communication style to match the people they're looking after.

Regardless of the tone of voice in which your personal guardian angel speaks to you, their message will come to you in a way that you perceive as one of love and compassion. Angels don't have egos, so they won't judge you or make you feel bad about yourself.

If you feel that you're receiving a message from an angel, but that message is harsh, unkind, or condemning, it's more likely your ego that you're hearing. Or it could be your own lack of self-forgiveness making itself heard. An angel simply won't speak to you in an unkind way.

SIGNS FROM YOUR ANGELS

Angels often send us signs that they are with us. Common signs from angels include seeing white butterflies, white feathers, pennies on the ground, and the number 4 over and over—most often as 444. Certain sequences of numbers hold specific meanings. Seeing 44 or 444 means "the angels are with you," which is a message people often receive when they have forgotten we are never alone.

Signs can also include "coincidences" that are in fact synchronicities—ways in which the angels are trying to get your attention. Let's say that you've learned the name of your guardian angel is Adam, but you're unsure whether to trust this information. If you suddenly encounter the name Adam multiple times the next day, then that is your confirmation that you heard your angel's name correctly! You might also turn on the radio to hear a song with lyrics that seem tailored to the challenges you are experiencing. The proof is around if you take a deeper look.

Here's a hypothetical example of the way angels can send signs. Imagine a couple who had to frequently travel down the 401 highway to see one other. They decide to get married, but a few weeks before their wedding, they are fretting because they can't find the perfect house to move into together. Just when it seems as if nothing will become available, they ask their angels to help them. Next time their real estate agent takes them to see a home, they begin to laugh, because the address is 401 Mason Lane. They know it's a sign that this is the right house for them!

WANT YOUR ANGELS' HELP? THEN YA HAFTA ASK!

Angels live not only to serve Source but also to serve humankind. However, because of free will, you must ask for an angel's assistance to get it. Think of angels as being on a fairly strict noninterference policy. If you don't ask for their help, then by and large, they must sit by the sidelines and watch. The only exception is that sometimes angels *can* intervene in someone's life without request in times of great emergency. We have plenty of evidence of stories where angels have done just that.

Once you request an angel's influence in a situation in your life, they can help out. So to begin working with angels, all you have to do is ask for their help and their messages. Do it every day.

I recommend starting with your guardian angels. The simplest way to begin a dialogue with your guardian angels is to find a quiet and still place. This can be out in nature or in your home. Try to choose a time when you can relax and will not be disturbed. Once you've settled in, take a few deep breaths and allow yourself to completely release any stress or any concerns that you have in the moment.

Either in your mind or aloud, say, "Hello, my name is _____. I know you're there guarding me and watching over me. And I know you know all that there is to know about me. However, I would like to know more of you. I would like to know your name."

If you suddenly feel that you've heard or sensed or just inexplicably "know" the answer, then that is your guardian angel's name. You may even experience more than one guardian angel at a time.

To help confirm what you've heard, you can say, "It would be very helpful to me to have a sign from you in the next 24 hours. If you could, please just send me a message of some sort so I can know we've communicated." Then be on the lookout for the common signs and synchronicities we discussed in the previous section.

If you don't connect right away with your angels, keep trying. It's like anything else; practice makes perfect. But definitely ask for their help every day—starting immediately. It might take some time for the communication to happen, but that doesn't mean they can't start to help you right away!

Once you've established a connection with your guardian angels, you can expand your angelic circle by reaching out to the archangels or special purpose angels that match what you want to create in your life.

MANIFESTING WITH THE ANGELS: PENNIES FROM HEAVEN

Working with the angels is a great way to manifest your dreams. If you do the work to create an active relationship with your guardian angels, they can give you advice on the right actions to take. The omnipresent archangels are also always available to you, especially if you take the time to learn their names and their specialties. Angelic guidance might come through signs or synchronicities that guide your actions. Or if you establish a dialogue with your angels through meditation, automatic writing, or by developing your clairaudience, you can receive direct messages.

Don't underestimate the ability of your angels to directly help you. I can't even begin to count the number of times I've asked my angels for a specific type of help or an outcome I had my heart set upon and they came through for me! It can be like "pennies from heaven!" I've also asked my angels for things that have *not* manifested and I was later grateful they didn't occur.

The more you work with the angels, the easier it becomes to have a dialogue and to recognize the touch of their loving care in your life.

AN ANGEL TO THE RESCUE!

Heather Hildebrand was a somewhat overwhelmed young woman who lived near Houston, Texas. One year, as usual, her plate was very full. She was joyously planning Thanksgiving dinner at her home and looking forward to welcoming out-of-town guests who were going to stay with her.

Heather had already gotten a great start on her Christmas planning. She'd even begun wrapping presents early. However, the cost of Heather's proactive attitude regarding the holidays was that the guest room was one huge mess. It had been a logical place to do her wrapping, but this led to the room becoming the dumping ground for all of the treasures Heather had found. There were bags scattered among neat piles of wrapped presents along the wall. Every inch of space was covered in bows, scissors, tape, and rolls of gift wrap.

With Thanksgiving closing in on her, Heather needed the room for her guests, and they would barely be able to wade through the sea of stuff. As she stood in the middle of this chaos she'd created for herself, Heather wondered how she'd muster the energy to clean all of it up. It was already way past midnight, and part of her wanted to just leave it and shut the door. But that wasn't an option.

So Heather took a deep breath and got to work. Soon, she was actually enjoying the peacefulness that these late hours offered, with the rest of her family tucked quietly in bed. Heather was almost done when she opened the door to an old armoire that had been passed down through her husband's family. As she reached in to hide some of the last bits of items that needed to be put away, something caught her eye.

Heather couldn't believe it when she spotted a royal blue photo album that she'd created for her father that held approximately 20 pictures. She hadn't seen it in years; as she pulled it out, her heart tingled. Heather's father had died 17 years prior, and the pictures that filled these pages were some of the last photos taken of him.

The gift had been her first attempt at scrapbooking and the last Father's Day gift she'd been able to give him. Heather flipped through the pages slowly, admiring every snapshot. Each photo had her son right there along with her father. The two of them had been the best of buddies, and Heather's dad had worried that his grandson would never remember him. That's why Heather created this amazing album for both grandfather and grandson.

At that moment, a thought entered Heather's mind that made her heart sink. She began to wonder if she'd ever truly grieved his death, although she'd never doubted the family's decision to take him off of life support. It was what he'd wanted, and God had given her peace at the time. She'd even been ready to let him go. So why was it that now she felt uncertainty when pondering if she'd truly grieved?

As Heather placed the album back into the armoire, she asked her angels, "Have I not grieved my father? Have I been avoiding the inevitable?" She asked her angels to give her a sign that she'd honored his memory through that grief process. "I know you're always with me and I'm so grateful for your love," Heather said. "Please help me to know without a shadow of a doubt that I'm okay. Please let me know that I'm not fooling myself."

Heather walked into the next room to throw away the trash, and as she turned around to leave, she suddenly felt as if she'd walked into a huge wall of love. There's absolutely no other way to describe it. There it was—her sign!

Heather was paralyzed by awe as she was presented with an enormous being of light about four feet away from her. It was a color that she couldn't really "see," but it "felt" golden in nature. Floating at least two feet from the floor, it was about two feet wide and three and a half feet tall.

Then suddenly, the light vanished. Gasping from shock, Heather hoped the figure might have jumped behind the wall into another room out of her sight. She wasn't really afraid, as she could feel that the angel's intention was to give her the answer she'd sought. She hurried around the corner, hoping to see its beauty again, but it was gone. However, the feeling of infinite love it left behind still filled the room.

Heather plopped herself down on the floor to try to enjoy every last drop of it. She felt almost drunk on this love that had been poured upon her. She considered sleeping right there, in that exact spot, in case this angel decided to show itself again. Eventually, Heather made her way downstairs to get ready for bed, but she still felt the goose bumps and amazement.

As Heather climbed into bed, she sent up the deepest prayers of gratitude her heart could gather. Her question had been answered loud and clear, and her worries had been put to rest.

"Thank you, angels," she whispered.

THE RAD-SCOOP ON WORKING WITH THE ANGELS

The type of people that I find angels work well for are those that have a strong system of faith. It's just naturally easier for these individuals to believe in any given spiritual discipline. People who are very openhearted and have natural psychic abilities that they've embraced and are willing to explore also do well with angels.

I like to call those who prefer working with angels "angel-folk." They tend to show angelic types of personalities. They are compassionate and always trying to help others. They might tend to put other's needs before their own. They are very loving people.

If you're the type where "seeing is believing," then you may have to work a bit harder to develop that faith. Looking for some of the common signs of angels in your life can help. If faith doesn't necessarily come easy to you, and it feels more natural to connect with academic or esoteric disciplines, angels may seem too ethereal.

I know extraordinarily gifted psychics who acknowledge the presence of angels but much prefer their charts and sciencelike astrology and numerology. Like I said, getting information from winged beings of light can just seem too "fluffy" for some people.

Why do *I* work so much with angels? Well, as I mentioned before, angels are a great place to begin to stretch our spiritual wings. As someone raised with a Southern religious background, I had a lot of fear to overcome. I started my personal exploration with angels, and my experience with them has been powerful, moving, and very real.

My relationships with my primary guardian angel, Joshua, as well as Archangels Uriel and Gabriel are deeply important to me and have provided me with a great many insights. I've made important changes in my life based upon their guidance, and those midcourse corrections have always taken me to greater joy and happiness in my life. And in the end . . .

I ♥ angels!

CHAPTER 3

THE MAGIC OF FAIRIES

IS WORKING WITH FAIRIES THE RIGHT CHOICE FOR YOU?

- Does being out in nature make you feel connected to something you can't see?

- Are you very concerned and active about protecting the environment?

- Are you naturally a playful person?

- Are your primary concerns at this time about manifesting material needs in your life?

Angels and fairies have some things in common, but they are ultimately very different from one another. There are people who are full-on members of "Team Angels" and others who will declare their allegiance to "Team Fairies" till the day they return to Source. Let's get some clarity on how these beings are alike and how they're different.

The vast majority of people who've developed a strong relationship with fairies believe them to be another form of life on earth that is just slightly out of phase with ours. Think of it like a radio station. If humans are accessible at 101.5, fairies might be found at 101.9. In other words, they're close, but they're not tuned in to the same frequency that humans are. Those who work with fairies and have developed their Divine gifts can change the channel just enough to experience and work with fairies. (By the way, this analogy doesn't really work with angels. Angels are not "of the earth," and so if we keep with this analogy, they're basically "not on the radio.")

Fairies can be quite charitable to humans. They are at least charitable to those humans they deem to be worthy of kindness. But don't confuse fairies and angels, because fairies are different from angels in the following ways:

- Angels are believed to exist to be of service to humankind, while fairies have more of an "I'll help you if I think you deserve it" sort of philosophy.

- While angels are of heaven, fairies are of the earth.

- Fairies may choose to help you manifest that which you want in life; however, they can also be tricksters whose sense of humor might play out at your expense.

- Fairies often want something in return for their good graces, whereas angels tend to give for the sake of giving.

- Fairies are most interested in the environment and animals, whereas angels are more focused on human beings.

- Fairies can see us, but we can't quite see them, because *they don't want to be seen.*

- Perhaps the most important difference between angels and fairies is that fairies have egos, while angels are just pure love. Those fairy egos are what have given fairies a reputation for playing tricks and wreaking havoc.

Some people won't believe in fairies at all, and that's just fine with the fairies. They know that the ability to perceive magic has been literally bred out of some human beings. These people prefer to live a very literal life, and it's very difficult for them to believe in something that might exist but just be slightly out of phase with our dimension.

Like angels, fairies *are* creatures of service. It's just that they're here to be of service to Mother Earth rather than humankind. If you're an environmentalist, chances are they'll be glad to be of assistance to you. And since they have you in their corner, they're probably going to give that assistance in a way that brings a smile or a little rush to your heart.

Never doubt that fairies take their mission seriously; they *will* get upset with those who thwart them. And remember that fairies have egos! If you're in the woods and you toss your organic green drink bottle on the ground because you're too lazy to find a trash can—well, you're not exactly making the fairies happy. They're extremely environmentally conscious, and they expect you to live in that way, too.

I'm often asked: "But Radleigh, why should I believe in these tricksters? And are they really tricksters?"

Yes, they can be tricksters, and they have that reputation. But to anyone who's actually seeking to work with fairies, the "tricks" almost always show up in a good-natured way. They're friendly and helpful to those who seek them out. Although as a species, I believe they're quite upset as they watch humans mess up the planet.

JUST A *LITTLE* HISTORY

First, a little fairy lingo for you: *Fairy* is also spelled *faery* in certain parts of the world. They are also referred to as "the fae."

The term *fairy* goes back to the Middle Ages in Europe. The oldest and most common stories about fairies come from Europe and the British Isles, though evidence of a belief in them can also be found in Asia, Africa, and the Americas. Tales of fairies include the nymphs of Greek mythology and the jinn from old Arabic. You can find them in stories from Arctic civilizations and even those of Native Americans.

Today, stories about fairies are strongest in Scotland, Ireland, Cornwall, and Wales. It's my experience that locals from these areas are reluctant to discuss fairies, leprechauns, or other mystical creatures with outsiders. However, if you inquire about them and voice your belief in their reality, these locals will suddenly open up and give you tons of information about where to find them and share their personal stories of interacting with the "wee folk."

Stories across cultures about the origins of fairies are . . . well . . . let's just say they're complicated! The tales are as diverse and contradictory as the cultures that created them. Some of the theories people have had about fairies include that they are:

- the souls of loved ones who've passed on
- another form of angels that protect nature and animals
- entities trapped between heaven and earth
- a form of ancient humans forced into hiding by invading forces
- another form of life altogether

Some stories about fairies describe them as being just slightly smaller than humans, and others say they're only inches high. There are tales that speak of fairies and humans having romantic relationships, though those stories rarely work out well for the human.

Fairies were usually said to live underground or in another dimension just out of view of our own. Some stories tell tales where humans who venture into the fairies' dimension have their wishes come true. Later, missing our world, the humans ask to be returned home, only to find many years have gone by—or conversely, only an instant has gone by—in our world while they've experienced several years in fairyland. Other tales say that if you eat or drink in fairyland, you're trapped there forever.

There are somewhat famous fairies who have special gifts. They're sort of like the fairy versions of archangels. Two of the most famous are Oberon, said to be the king of the fairies, and his consort, Titania, queen of the fairies.

SO YOU WANT TO MEET THE FAIRIES . . .

You see a flash of light whiz by; you blink and it's gone. Out of the corner of your eye, you see sparkles but can't figure out why. You've spent your walk along the beach picking up trash purely out of love for the planet, and when you walk back to the parking lot, there's a $50 bill just lying next to your car. These are all experiences of encountering a fairy.

To actually *see* fairies, you have to get to a point where, after much practice, you're able to shift yourself to see their energy. I strongly urge those who wish to make these kinds of connections to do so in nature. Great places to make contact with fairies are in the woods, in the mountains, by a river, in a park, or even in your own backyard.

Try to find yourself a lovely spot outdoors. Allow yourself to get into a restful, meditative space, but allow your eyes to remain open. Try not to focus on any one thing, just let your gaze kind of wander. Without exerting undue effort, try to notice what you see out of the corners of your eyes. Look for little sparkles of light. Now softly ask that these sparkles of light spend time with you. You can speak aloud or just in your own mind. Ask for what you would like to create in your life and for their assistance in it.

Then, before you leave, do a little work around your spot in nature. Clean up any litter. Water some flowers, put out some birdseed, or otherwise see to the needs of Mother Nature. Try to keep yourself mindful of those sparkles of light and where they are around you.

Remember that fairies want to be of assistance to humans whom they deem worthy of such help. And similarly, they may wish to be rewarded for their efforts. Some people put out little sweet treats for fairies, such as fresh fruit or chocolates. As fairies are considered to be of the earth, others concern themselves with things like recycling or volunteering with agencies focused on conservation and kindness to animals to win the good will of fairies.

MANIFESTING WITH THE FAIRIES: MAGIC FOR THE FAE-THFUL

Fairies are amazing manifesters, and they're particularly good about manifesting "stuff." Need a new car? Information might just show up about an amazing deal from somewhere you weren't expecting. Need a new couch? Someone might be wanting to give away one that's practically brand new. Need a raise?

You see where I'm going with this. And don't worry—it's so simple! All you need to do is ask the fairies for what you want to be manifested, and do not worry about details or the outcome.

For their help with manifesting what *you* want, fairies want something in return. They want your help protecting Mother Earth and her beautiful creatures. So do some charity work, donate to proven organizations, or just do your part to clean up while on a walk through nature.

Another thing that'll get you on the fairy "good girl" or "good boy" list is making a place for fairies in your garden. Find an out-of-the-way spot that won't be disturbed. Leave small sweets and fruits for them there, but make sure what you put out is safe for your pets. (For example, don't leave chocolate where your pooch can get it.) Plant flowers that attract butterflies. Some people even create little fairylands in a corner of their garden, complete with little fairy houses and toadstools.

Show the fairies you want their assistance and you're on their side.

Oh. And you have to believe.

FOLLOWING TINKER BELL

On a beautiful late summer evening, Wendy Preis was returning home from her new job. Just a month into her new career, she was still learning to navigate through all the towns between her home and the office, so she really only knew one route to take.

On this particular evening, it had rained pretty hard, and the small streams and rivers near where Wendy lived were filling up fast; some were even overflowing into the streets. Wendy was forced to take many detours on the way home, going through towns she'd never driven through before.

Her normally 30-minute drive home grew until it felt like she'd been driving for hours. As the sun set and Wendy's car continued to use up its fuel, she began to panic. Her heart raced as she realized she truly had no idea where she was, and she had no money or credit cards on her to get more gas.

It was now raining very hard, and Wendy was overcome by eerie feelings as she drove through towns she didn't recognize. She wasn't the most emotional person under normal circumstances, but suddenly she burst into tears and couldn't stop. The waterworks just kept coming and coming. She didn't feel safe enough to pull over to ask for directions, and there were no gas stations in sight. When the low fuel indicator light on her car blinked on, Wendy began to cry harder.

That's when Wendy remembered a class she'd taken a year before about manifesting with Mother Earth and the inhabitants of the elemental kingdoms such as fairies. She called out to Mother Earth and the fairies in a terrified but very loving way: "Please, please, please help me find my way home!" she asked. As she said aloud this a few times, an overwhelming calmness flowed through her. Seemingly from out of nowhere, an old beat-up car pulled out in front of Wendy.

The rain beating down on the windshield made it difficult to see, but with each swish of the wipers, Wendy's tear-filled eyes were drawn to the car in front of her. She suddenly had an overwhelming sense to just follow. This inner knowing was telling Wendy that no matter which way this car turned, she should keep following. Several minutes later, she started to get the sense that she was in familiar territory. The rain was slowly subsiding, and her view was becoming clearer. She now knew the way home!

Wendy then took a closer look to see exactly who she'd been so faithfully following. To her utter surprise and delight, it was a red Volkswagen Rabbit covered with Tinker Bell stickers! Wendy also noticed that there was a bumper sticker that said *Be good to Mother Earth. Recycle.* But the truly amazing thing was the license plate: FOL-OM3." Everything about the car basically shouted out "Follow Me!"

THE RAD-SCOOP ON WORKING WITH THE FAIRIES

People who have an innate ability to believe in what's unseen will probably do better in working with fairies than those who find faith a challenge. In fact, most of the people I know who work with fairies also believe in angels, and vice versa. I definitely believe in fairies, even though I prefer working with angels.

Many who prefer fairy work tend to be less "angelic" and more fairylike themselves. If your nature tends to be more playful, you may be more drawn to fairies. You probably don't sweat the small stuff, and you have a tendency to see the frivolity of life. This personality type complements fairy work because with the fae, you're never quite sure what you're going to get. If you tend to be mischievous and rebellious, or you find yourself with strong judgments about how others should behave, then you may find the energy of fairies is more in alignment with yours than the energy of angels is. Fairies have a very definite view of right and wrong. If you're someone who waffles, then you might work better with a different belief system.

If there's something that you're wishing for (particularly something material), then you might want to call upon the fairies. Fairies are very good at manifesting and have a magical ability to make things appear.

If you like to pick up other people's trash for no real reason, are at peace sitting in a tree or going on a hike, or are always the one insisting on grabbing a kayak to hit the water, then you might be a prime candidate to embrace fairies, because they're just naturally found in those places.

What do I think? I used to be more in tune with fairies than I am now. I still do absolutely believe in fairies. Working with the fairies can be hugely rewarding and tremendously fun, so long as you remember who you're dealing with and hold up your side of the bargain by treating Mother Earth like the classy lady she is.

That being said, I'm just naturally more of an angel boy. As I told you in Chapter 2, I have been since I was five years old.

CHAPTER 4

THE MAGIC OF TAROT AND ORACLE CARDS

ARE TAROT AND ORACLE CARDS THE RIGHT CHOICE FOR YOU?

- Do you believe in the power of intuition and psychic gifts but have trouble accessing or believing in your own abilities?
- Are you a very visual person with a creative imagination?
- Do you find joy in symbolism and imagery?

One of the things I'm most known for is tarot—in particular, taking the fear out of the imagery and interpretation of tarot for people who found it worrisome. At the time of this book's writing, I've created five tarot decks and one deck of oracle cards, and have another two tarot decks in process. I won't embarrass myself by telling you how many decks I own; the number is completely absurd. It's safe to say that I've committed a considerable amount of my life to teaching people about the amazing world of tarot and oracle cards—so let's get started!

Tarot is an ancient divinatory tool using images on cards that are approximately the same size and structure as ordinary playing cards. There are 78 cards broken up into the Minor Arcana and the Major Arcana. *Arcana* means "secrets" or "mysteries," so they're basically the "little mysteries" and the "big mysteries."

The 56 cards of the Minor Arcana contain four suits that correlate closely with regular playing cards. Traditionally, these four suits are Wands, Cups, Swords, and Coins (or Pentacles), but many tarot authors have played with those suit names to make them thematic or less frightening. (Guilty!) Each of these four suits contains 14 cards: 10 "pip cards" (ace through 10) and four court cards (usually a Page, a Knight, a Queen, and a King). An additional 22 cards make up a kind of "fifth suit" of the Major Arcana. They depict a story of the major events in life.

If you come across a card deck that deviates from this specific formula of 78 cards made up of the Major and Minor Arcanas, you've left the Land of Tarot and have entered Oracle City! Oracle cards operate on the same principal as tarot cards but without the traditional structure. These decks can comprise as many or as few cards as the creator desires. Each card has its own unique name, symbolism, and imagery. Oracle decks generally do not contain suits, pip cards, or court cards, and the majority of them aren't even numbered. It's that simple!

There are oracle decks built around every subject you can possibly imagine. For example, some cards are built around specific types of art, calling upon the energy of specific entities like fairies or angels, or to assist with a specific tasks such as finding your life purpose or romance. Some decks are very serious, while others are more whimsical in nature with themes like kittens or puppies. Keep in mind that just because a deck has a light-hearted theme, you can still get very deep and powerful messages from it.

Both tarot and oracle decks come with a guidebook where you'll find expanded meanings written about each of the cards.

In order to make oracle cards even simpler to use, they often come with key words or phrases printed right on the cards. This alleviates the need to memorize the meanings in the guidebook and can assist those who are just starting to use the decks to get answers very quickly. However, these same beneficial key words can be a detriment to some people who may find it hard to look past those phrases for deeper meanings and conclusions.

It's arguable that tarot provides more detailed answers to your questions than oracle cards, but both have an important place as languages of the Divine. I love them both.

JUST A *LITTLE* HISTORY

The Major and Minor Arcanas of tarot did not begin as a combined deck. At some point, two separate decks became partnered as tarot.

The earliest evidence of card decks combining the Major and Minor Arcanas dates back to early 15th-century Italy. The cards were created as a parlor game called Tarocchi. They were hand created by artists and were usually owned only by those wealthy enough to commission their own decks. By the early 16th century, the decks were much more widely distributed throughout Italy and France, with the center of French production being in Marseilles. While the basic construction of the decks was fairly consistent (four suits plus a fifth suit of trump cards), the order of the cards inside the deck tended to vary between manufacturers.

There's some evidence that tarot was used for divination during its early years. However, its true popularity as such a tool really took off in the 18th and 19th centuries when it was discovered by spiritualists. An organization call the Hermetic Order of the Golden Dawn became particularly enthralled with the potential symbolism in the cards. Aspects of astrology, numerology, and Kabbalah were all attributed to the cards—particularly to the Major Arcana.

It was during this time that stories began to emerge connecting tarot to everything from ancient Egypt to Moses and other lofty spiritual sources. Sadly, there's no evidence for such associations except for starry-eyed dreaming (and even some plain old lying!).

The same people that became so enamored with tarot as a divination tool also had a tendency to shroud it in secrecy, explaining the symbolism attributed to each card only to initiates of their organizations. This made the deck of cards seem mysterious and even frightening to those who weren't privy to how they worked.

In the early 1900s, tarot scholar Arthur Edward Waite partnered up with artist Pamela Colman Smith to create what's arguably the most famous tarot deck in the entire world. The first publisher of the deck was Rider and Company of London; hence, the deck is most often called the Rider-Waite deck. However, many modern-day scholars refer to this deck as the Waite-Smith deck in order to give credit to the considerable contributions made by the artist.

The Rider-Waite/Waite-Smith deck was notable for having detailed imagery on the pip cards. Prior to this time, almost all pip cards in tarot decks just looked like ordinary playing cards, displaying the usual seven cups or nine wands, for example, on each card. The inclusion of symbolic illustrations with people interacting with each other or active with some task was a huge transformation for tarot.

Since that time, countless versions of tarot decks have been created. Some of them are very serious and maintain a close relationship to traditional tarot, while other decks are more whimsical. Some decks deviate greatly from historical tarot. For example, they might leave out the court cards or add cards to the Major Arcana. Those works that drift far from convention I tend to refer to as "tarot oracle" decks.

TAKING THE FEAR OUT OF TAROT

Everywhere I go, I run into people who are either intimidated by or just outright terrified of tarot cards. "It's so scary," people will tell me. "The images just seem so dark, and I can't use them."

It pains me to hear these fears, but tarot has been given something of a reputation by its roles in movies and television. It's easy to conclude that the whole thing is shrouded in secrecy and perhaps involves strange symbols and spooky fortune-tellers who hold power over the fate of the people who come to see them. Some may worry that those intricate, scary-looking cards will be filled with inescapable bad news.

For many, tarot seems to have an inherent mystery to it. I can understand that perception. Early tarot decks were, in fact, quite mysterious and obscure. Even the images were pretty murky and were only clear to those schooled in metaphysical studies. Some of the imagery can seem violent in nature by today's sensibilities. This can create a situation where people shun tarot because they basically "don't want to know what they don't know."

Complicating matters even more is that a lot of the cards don't mean what they seem to mean at first glance. For instance, let's take the Death card, which can understandably shake some people to the core. Many avoid tarot, thinking, *What if my reader pulls the Death card? Will I die? Should I just go home and hide under the covers? Is my life over?* That's absolutely not the case!

Let me assure you that 99.9 percent of the time, the Death card doesn't mean death. It usually says something about the end of a *situation* rather than the end of a life. I've been working with tarot for 30 years and I've only seen a reading tell of an impending end of life once, and the spread didn't involve the Death card at all.

Another scary card for many is the devilish-looking one, which doesn't mean that evil spirits are about to invade your bedroom late at night. Instead, tarot readers know that this card actually indicates a fixation with materialistic concerns like money, wealth, and power. It may also refer to self-imposed imprisonment, like an addiction that might need treatment.

The imagery and names of traditional tarot cards were created many hundreds of years ago. Those pictures and words were seen differently in the 15th and 16th centuries. All of this is why

I took it as part of my life purpose to bring tarot into the 21st century. I removed all those gruesome images and scary words from my own tarot decks and replaced them with words that matched the *true* meaning of the cards. I also placed words on the cards so that anyone could see what a card meant without a lot of memorization and secrecy. All of life's ups and downs are still there—just without the utterly unnecessary blood and gore.

TALKING TO YOURSELF

Part of what makes tarot and oracle cards work is that they tap into the subconscious. That's the part of ourselves that can look at the imagery and the written meanings of the cards and connect with our own innate intuition. I believe anyone can read the cards in a very analytical way based on the intellectual study of their meaning and come up with some fascinating and accurate results.

However, the amazing truths and real answers to our questions and concerns show up when we place our analytical selves aside, thus allowing Divine wisdom to come through. In this place of nonjudgment, answers will well up from the depths of our hearts and souls, and from these messages we can be enlightened, inspired, and healed.

The other reason these decks work is faith. Tarot has been around for so very long, with so many people placing their own energy and trust into it, that it's come to have a power of its own. Consider the recent breakthroughs in quantum physics that show that our beliefs fuel reality. Belief in the conscious creation of what happens in our lives via positive intention has reignited in the spiritual community.

If you believe that humanity is creating a common reality by all of us believing in the same general experience of life on earth, then you can also see how millions of people over hundreds of years believing in tarot might empower the cards and their use as a divinatory tool.

READING THE CARDS

In order to begin working with cards, you will naturally need a deck! My suggestion is always that people visit a store in person to choose your cards, either a metaphysical shop or bookstore. A metaphysical shop will likely have many different decks for you to choose from. Usually, there are sample decks that allow you to look through the cards, hold them in your hands, and get a feel for their energy. Sadly, brick and mortar bookstores are becoming less and less common. So if visiting an actual shop isn't possible, then turn to the Internet. Do an online search for recent and popular "tarot cards" or "oracle cards," and look at the images that turn up.

As you look through a particular deck, whether online or in a store, notice how the cards make you feel. Do you feel happy? Intrigued? Uncomfortable? Nothing at all? Choose a deck that resonates with you emotionally.

Once you have your cards, follow the instructions for clearing and consecrating the cards found in the section "Preparing to Work with Your Oracles" in Chapter 1. I would suggest you also use the reading prayer also found in that section (or one of your own making) before starting to work with the cards.

Pick up the cards and begin to shuffle them while you think of the question you are seeking an answer to. There is no right or wrong way to shuffle the cards. Some people just slowly take sections of the cards out of the deck and then mix them back into the deck. People say I shuffle like I'm at a poker table in a casino! It doesn't matter how you do it. Just follow your own Divine guidance.

The simplest way to do a card reading is to ask your question while shuffling the cards, then pull a single card. The Law of Attraction will ensure that you pull the right card to shed light on the situation you're concerned about.

If one or more cards "jump" out of the deck while you're shuffling, place them to the side. They'll be part of your reading, adding context outside the meanings in the spread.

As you're shuffling, you'll likely notice accompanying feelings, thoughts, words, or visions. These inner messages will help you understand the cards you draw, so pay attention to everything that you feel, think, hear, and see.

You may also receive a feeling or a "knowing" to stop shuffling the cards, or you might even hear the words *Stop shuffling now*. Again, the Law of Attraction ensures that you'll always be guided to the correct cards so you can't make a mistake and stop too soon. Set aside your worries or fears about doing it wrong.

Once you stop shuffling, pull any card from the deck. Some people pull the card on top. Other people fan out the cards and choose the one that seems to call to them. Again, there is no right or wrong way to do this. However, decide which way you're are going to choose the card before you begin the process. By setting the intention ahead of time, you allow the Law of Attraction to move the cards to the right place in the deck.

The card you draw is always the right one, so don't worry about choosing incorrectly. Whichever card you pull is the answer to your question. If the deck you have chosen has words on it, read the message. Notice any additional words, thoughts, feelings, or visions that come to you as you read the message on the card. The picture on the card is important as well. Notice where your eyes go when you look at it, and pay attention to how you feel. Everything you see and feel is part of the answer to your question.

If you set aside a card (or cards) that "jumped" out of the deck while you were shuffling, look at it too.

After looking at the images and examining your feelings, be sure to look at the card's meaning in the guidebook if your tarot or oracle deck came with one. Guidebooks are a great way to start learning about the cards. However, in time, you'll learn that guidebooks are just that—a guide. It is not the beginning and end of what a card can mean. In the end, the card means what your intuition tells you it means. Your Divine guidance will always bear more weight in a reading than what a guidebook tells you.

SPREADING THE MAGIC AROUND

To do more complex readings, you'll be pulling several cards and laying them out in a specific pattern, or "spread." Spreads enhance and add context to the cards you choose by imbuing meaning into the placement of each card.

For example, look at Figure 4.1, which is a very simple three-card spread.

Figure 4.1. Three-card spread

- **Card 1:** Information from the past that led to the situation you're asking about.

- **Card 2:** The present, where things stand right now.

- **Card 3:** The future, or the most likely outcome if no changes in action are taken.

One of the most popular and beloved card spreads in tarot, the Celtic Cross can be used to answer questions about any topic. (See Figure 4.2.) This spread of 10 cards reveals the basis of the situation you inquired about, the challenge, the past, the present, the near future, and the likely outcome.

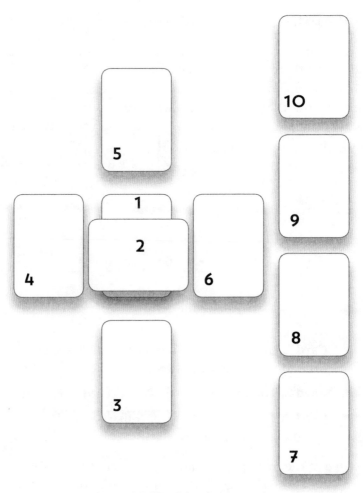

Figure 4.2. The Celtic Cross spread

- **Card 1:** The present moment. The primary concern.
- **Card 2:** The challenge affecting Card 1. A block. The cause of the challenge.
- **Card 3:** Subconscious influences. Unknown information. The distant past.

- **Card 4:** The recent past. A situation that has come to a conclusion.

- **Card 5:** The present. Conscious beliefs. Current events.

- **Card 6:** The near future. A new person or event. A shift in energy.

- **Card 7:** Your power (or lack of power) in the moment. How you see yourself in the situation.

- **Card 8:** The effects of people around you. How other people see you in the situation.

- **Card 9:** Your hopes or fears.

- **Card 10:** The most likely outcome.

It's important to note that some decks are created with the intention that cards that are pulled from the deck upside down, or "reversed," have a different meaning than cards that are pulled upright. Other authors of decks might ask you to simply turn the card upside right and read it that way but give that card particular emphasis in the reading. Which way a specific deck asks that you treat reversed cards should be addressed in the guidebook that comes with the cards.

People often misunderstand reversed cards as thinking that they mean the opposite of what the card would represent if it were not reversed, but that is usually not the case. For example, if the card you've pulled means "good luck," it doesn't necessarily mean "bad luck" if it's upside down. It's more likely it would mean the diminishing of the energy of the good luck. Just because a time of great good fortune is passing doesn't mean you're headed into a time of bad fortune. You might just be moving toward a more average time in your life.

There are plenty of spreads to choose from, ranging from the very simple to the complex, in various books and on the Internet. I recommend my own book, *The Big Book of Angel Tarot*, or you can check out the recommended reading section at the back of this book.

MANIFESTING WITH TAROT AND ORACLE CARDS: STACKING THE DECK IN YOUR FAVOR

There are several ways to manifest with a tarot or oracle deck. The simplest is to select a card from the deck that reflects the energy of what you want to bring in. Interested in a financial windfall? You might pull out the Ace of Earth (or Coins). Need some healing in your relationship? Choose the Two of Water (or Cups). If you're using an oracle card deck, you can pick whatever card speaks to your specific need.

Whatever card you choose, carry it with you. Reflect upon the card many times a day. If you have an altar at home, you might place the card on the altar. Hold the card while meditating and ask the card for advice to come through during your meditations.

Another way I teach for manifesting with cards is to amp up the energy of the card with a crystal that carries the right energy. For example, pyrite and green jade are stones known for their ability to bring prosperity. Placing either or both of those stones on the Ace of Earth or Coins increases the energy of the card and focuses the energy of the crystals on your goal of bringing in abundance.

MAYBE YOU SHOULD TAKE A HOME TAROT TEST

Mandy, one of my favorite clients, came to me to discuss her desire to have a baby. It turned out that she and her husband had been trying to have a child for a while without success.

"Maybe I'm blocking what I want the most in life," she told me, confiding her deepest fear. "Do you have any idea what I can do and when I might become pregnant?"

At that time in my life, I knew nothing about pregnancy and babies. But I did believe in the power of tarot, which I knew could help provide some insight into Mandy's concerns. To that end, I laid out a spread of cards. Once I did, I couldn't contain my smile. I wasn't about to tell her that her pregnancy would happen this year, this quarter, or even this month.

"Mandy, you're *already* pregnant!" I said.

As I said those words, she looked up in utter shock. "Oh, no!" she said. "I'm quite sure I'm not pregnant. I just took a home pregnancy test yesterday, and it was negative."

"Go take another one," I instructed her.

The next day, she basically floated back into my office. "Oh my God! You were so right! I'm pregnant!"

Then she added, "Do you know the sex of my child?"

After making sure that this was information she really wanted to know, I looked to the cards again.

Eight months later, as I told her she would, she welcomed a healthy baby boy.

That is the power of tarot.

THE RAD-SCOOP ON TAROT AND ORACLE CARDS

It should come as no surprise that I have a deep love affair with tarot. I've been using the cards for nearly 30 years and they've provided me with great epiphanies, comfort, and guidance. I've also read cards for countless people over the years, and I can tell you that they've brought hope to the hopeless, direction to the lost, and joy to the downhearted more times that I could possibly count.

The decks that I've created have made it much easier for people to pick up a deck and start using it right away. Blending angels and fairies into the decks dispels a lot of fear and allows people to see just how much help tarot can be in their lives.

The truth about tarot and oracle cards is that those who truly believe in themselves could get the same insights from their own Divine intuition. Sadly, most people don't have faith in their inner guidance. Tarot and oracle cards give them a way to bring that guidance out into the open where they can access it. In short, they may not believe in themselves, but they do believe in the cards. Which is so very ironic, since the cards are only mirroring what's within them.

CHAPTER 5

THE MAGIC OF THE LENORMAND

IS THE LENORMAND THE RIGHT CHOICE FOR YOU?

- Do you like to consult an oracle for answers to day-to-day questions?

- Would you prefer a small deck of cards in both size and number?

- Do you prefer conversational messages rather than deeply symbolic ones?

- Do you have a great memory? (Because you'll need one.)

The Lenormand is a set of 36 cards used for divination. While tarot, oracle, and Lenormand cards can all give you answers about any question, whether deeply spiritual or mundane, some see tarot as more for the deeply spiritual and the Lenormand as more for daily life.

The cards are usually small in size—smaller even than regular playing cards—because spreads tend to be quite large. In fact, the most famous spread for the Lenormand uses all 36 cards.

Each card is considered to be either positive, neutral, or negative. However, as in tarot, context is everything; a card that is generally considered to be negative might be quite positive in the right position, sitting next to the right cards.

The 36 cards of the Lenormand in their traditional order (with commentary by me) are Rider, Clover, Ship, House, Tree, Clouds, Snake *(ew)*, Coffin *(double ew)*, Bouquet, Scythe, Whip, Birds, Child, Fox, Bear, Stars, Stork, Dog, Tower, Garden, Mountain, Crossroads, Mice, Heart, Ring, Book, Letter, Man, Woman, Lilies, Sun, Moon, Key, Fish, Anchor, and Cross.

Actually, the Lenormand is *usually* and *historically* 36 cards. For several reasons, many modern decks have more than that.

Within a traditional deck, there's one card for Man and one card for Woman. Often in readings, the card that matches the gender of the person getting a reading is looked at as representing them in the spread. That's called a significator. The card of the opposite gender might represent their spouse or a best friend or close relative. In many contemporary Lenormand decks, there are two cards for Man and two cards for Woman to allow for same-sex relationships or just to allow the person getting a reading to pick the card of their gender that they feel more represents them. So that brings us up to 38 cards.

There's also a card called Child. Again, there might be a male and a female child in the deck if that is important to the question. Now we're up to 39 cards.

Some deck creators have added their own cards. In fact, the Lenormand deck that I most resonated with had 44 cards! Lenormand purists seem to be fine with the additional gender cards, but they are not so happy about added cards with nontraditional meanings.

Like tarot, the Lenormand has historical aspects that are associated with a parlor game. And while tarot and the Lenormand are both card decks used for divination, they're very different oracles. Whereas each tarot card has a singular meaning, the Lenormand delivers its messages via *combinations* of cards. Pulling a single card for a reading, as you can do with tarot and oracle decks, isn't generally done with the Lenormand.

The Lenormand tells a story; the cards are much like words in a sentence. Each card has many meanings, some of them only vaguely related to one another. On top of it all, the order of the cards in a spread completely changes the reading. If you pulled the cards Key, Dog, and Bouquet, the message would be completely different than if the cards order was Bouquet, Dog, and Key. To give you an idea of how this works, take the words in the sentence *That class is real* as an example. If you rearrange the words to *That is real class*, you'll see how the same word can refer to either a course or to elegance, depending on order.

Traditionally, every Lenormand card has a reference to a regular playing card. Of course, there are 52 cards in a poker deck but only 36 in the Lenormand. In the Lenormand, all of the twos, threes, fours and fives are removed. This is similar to another parlor game that was created in the 1600s called Piquet, which used regular playing cards with the twos through sixes removed to leave 32 cards.

Some decks (especially very old ones) have a picture of a playing card on the face of the Lenormand card along with the usual illustration that complements the card name. For example, you might see an image of the Nine of Clubs on the Fox card or the Queen of Diamonds on the Crossroads card. More contemporary sets of cards might have a reference to the playing cards in the corner without displaying the entire image—something like 9♣ or Q♦.

Naturally, the Lenormand has a connection to cartomancy, which is the reading of playing cards for divination. For advanced users of the Lenormand, cartomancy references become a part of the reading. The challenging aspect is that the meanings of the playing cards on the Lenormand cards do not correspond directly to traditional cartomancy.

JUST A *LITTLE* HISTORY

The tale of the Lenormand takes a lot of twists and turns, and the historical documents can contradict one another. Compared to the other oracles in this compendium, the Lenormand is a newborn. The first deck of cards was offered in the early 1800s, so the oracle is "only" a little over 200 years old.

The cards are named for Mlle Marie Anne Lenormand—even though she had nothing to do with their creation. (*Mlle* is the abbreviation for the French word *mademoiselle*.) Mlle Lenormand was a very famous fortune-teller (as she described herself) in France in the early 1800s. She was said to have been the card reader for Napoleon Bonaparte's wife, Empress Josephine, as well as for many other famous folks. Her fame was so widespread that when she passed away, her name was placed on all kinds of products that she had no involvement with.

The card game that the Lenormand is based upon was called the Game of Hope and was actually "created" by a German man named Johann Hechtel. I place the word *created* in quotation marks because there's strong evidence that he took the symbols for the cards directly from a book on how to read coffee grounds as a divination tool. Hechtel passed away right before the Game of Hope was published in 1799. When Mlle Lenormand passed away in 1843, the publisher renamed the game Le Petit Lenormand as a way to take advantage of her great fame, marketing it as her "secret oracle."

Whether Mlle Lenormand ever used the Game of Hope cards that would eventually be renamed for her is doubtful. She is thought to have primarily been a cartomancer, using regular playing cards as her divination tool. There are some references that suggest she may have used Piquet, but that isn't the same as actually having laid hands on the cards that would eventually bear her name.

SECOND VERSE, SAME AS THE FIRST

While the methodology and construction of the Lenormand is quite different from tarot or oracle cards, the *way* they work is virtually the same. (See "Talking to Yourself" in the previous chapter.) The imagery and meanings of the cards are read through intuition, and perhaps a bit of the subconscious, to get messages from the Divine.

THE LENORMAND LANGUAGE

Most authors and teachers of the Lenormand will tell you that it's very easy to learn, but I'm not sure I agree with that. The Lenormand requires a great deal of memorization, and some of it is challenging. To successfully do a reading, you'll first need to have memorized all of the meanings for each card.

Here's a typical example showing *just a few* of the possible meanings of the Lenormand card Stars: hope, dreams, inspiration, universe, recognition, antiseptic, psychic, Divine guidance, and electricity. Some of these meanings make sense and are related to one another. But antiseptic and electricity?

In the books I consulted, the minimum number of words listed for the meaning of Stars was 45. Multiply that times 36 cards and that's a *lot* to learn. (And for all you tarot lovers out there, don't think that just because the Lenormand has a few similar cards—Stars, the Sun, the Moon, and the Tower—that the cards have similar meanings. There is some crossover, but it's not at all the same.)

Then, once you've memorized the meanings of each card, you'll need to figure out what their meanings mean in relation to each other. Let's say that you want to ask the cards, "Should I write a book?" You shuffle the deck and pull out the cards Key, Book, and Ring.

In the Lenormand, the Key represents good fortune, the unlocking of opportunity, and breakthroughs (among many other things). The Book can be wisdom, secrets, or literally a book. Finally, among the many meanings for the Ring is a contract. The natural conclusion is, "Yes! You should write a book! It'll be a big success and will get you a publishing contract."

Now, I purposefully made this a very simple example to show you how the Lenormand works. My experience with this oracle is rarely that specific to any particular question. However,

I have always been able to piece things together to get an answer that made sense to me.

Spreads in the Lenormand are very similar to those used in tarot and oracle-card readings. Although some spreads are used more often for one type of card than another, the general concept remains the same.

The Lenormand's most famous spread, the Grand Tableau, is absolutely fascinating. It uses *all* of the cards in the deck, and there are so many ways in which cards on one side of the spread can relate to cards on the other side of the spread to tell a story. It's usually laid out as four rows of eight cards stacked on top of each other with the final four cards in the fifth row.

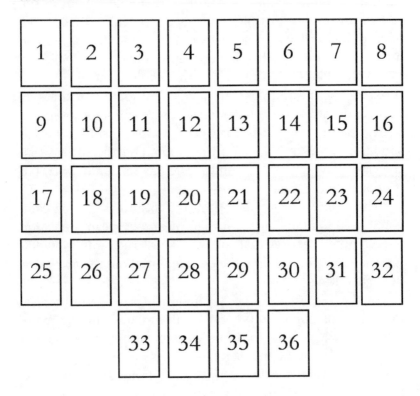

Figure 5.1. The Grand Tableau

Plenty of information is usually extracted from a Grand Tableau reading. For this spread, it's helpful to have the card order memorized even though the numbers are on the cards. If you know something about astrology (Chapter 9), then you'll be familiar with the concept of houses. There's a similar concept in the Lenormand Grand Tableau.

As an example, let's say that the Garden card has landed on the 14th position, or "house," in the spread. The Garden card represents crowds, parties, and events. Just as in astrology, the house has a certain energy to it that matches Lenormand card 14, the Fox. Among other things, Fox represents work, career, and employment. So the Garden card sitting in the 14th house (Fox energy) might represent something like a business conference or an office party.

MANIFESTING WITH THE LENORMAND: WRITING YOUR OWN STORY

Manifesting with the Lenormand is much like manifesting with tarot or oracle cards. The primary difference is that while you might carry or meditate on a single tarot card, that's not the way the Lenormand works. The Lenormand is about taking several cards and reading the story like a sentence. So when choosing Lenormand cards for this purpose, you need to pick cards to create a sentence or message for yourself that you want to manifest. For example, if you're trying to manifest a new romance, you might choose Rider (new love interest,) Bouquet (blooming relationship,) and House (stable relationship or moving in together).

RIGHT ON THE MONEY!

Professional tarot and Lenormand reader Andrew Barker remembers his first time working with these cards. As he told me in his own words:

I had just bought my first Lenormand deck, and I had no idea what to do with it. I bought it because of the art! However, I was interested in learning more about it, so I watched a lot of online videos about different card spreads and meanings and got a book or two as well.

After getting the gist of it, I decided I wanted to practice a bit to see if I was retaining what I'd learned and just to see what came through. I posted on my personal Facebook page that I wanted to do free practice readings, and within seconds I had over 10 comments from volunteers!

I was already kind of nervous. Having read tarot for a few years, I knew this was *very* different. However, one of my Facebook friends messaged me, and I agreed to give them a reading. They asked about their career, so I shuffled the cards, asked the specific question, and drew the Bear and the Fish.

Based on what I'd learned and the context of the question, I knew the Bear was talking about management and the Fish referred to abundance and prosperity. So I told my friend that a management opportunity was coming up for them. They seemed a bit hesitant but thanked me for my time.

Shortly after that, I received a message from my friend that their manager was going on vacation. They were going to take over the management role and get paid more during that time.

The Lenormand was right on the money!

THE RAD-SCOOP ON THE LENORMAND

In general, I've found the Lenormand to be enchanting. I love that it's simple yet also very complex. Like tarot, the cards are now available in a dizzying array of styles and themes. Finding the right deck was key for me, as the old 1800s images just left me flat. But once I found something contemporary and lush, I was totally fascinated. Honestly, I am charmed by the Lenormand.

That being said, it's a *lot* of memorization. If you have the time for a lot of practice and learning all the card meanings, what the combinations of the cards mean, and all the magical ways these cards interweave with one another, then I highly recommend the Lenormand.

Personally, I wish *I* had the time, because I would be all over it.

CHAPTER 6

THE MAGIC OF RUNES

ARE RUNES THE RIGHT CHOICE FOR YOU?

- Do you enjoy deep conversations?

- Are you wanting to understand yourself more fully?

- Do you seek spiritual insights to help you make choices more than trying to get glimpses of the future?

- Are you intrigued by an oracle that is small enough to take anywhere?

- Do you like the feel and look of crystals and pretty stones?

Runes are a system of 24 symbols (or 25, depending on who you ask) that historically were carved into wood or stone. There were several different versions of runes throughout Europe— some even became alphabets! The most common version (and the one most used as an oracle today) is called the Elder Futhark. While the Futhark never became an alphabet, letters were still ascribed to each symbol. F-U-T-H-A-R-K are the first six letters of the symbols in the order most people consider the runes to naturally flow. Just as the Major Arcana of tarot has an order, so too do the runes, though there are debates here and there about that order.

The runes are broken into groups, almost like the suits in tarot. These are groups of eight known as the *aettir* (pronounced "ett-teer"). Each group is referred to as an *aett* (pronounced "ett") and named for a Norse god or goddess. The first group is called Freyr's aett, then there's Hagal's aett, and finally Tyr's aett.

If you've been doing math in your head, you're noticing that we're now at 24 runes. There's one rune that stands alone: Wyrd (pronounced "weird"). This is a blank rune. *Wyrd* is an Old English word that means "fate." Its inclusion as a rune is a modern addition; many find it to be very controversial. Some traditional rune casters won't even use it in readings.

Serious rune casters often make their own runes in order to infuse their own energy into the symbols. Although rune makers still exist today who'll make a set specifically for you, more often people purchase them at stores and then clear them. (Directions for clearing can be found in Chapter 1.)

Runes often are carved on crystals or stones such as rose quartz or amethyst, making them lovely to look at and to hold. Usually they're kept in a little pouch that makes them easy to carry around with you.

JUST A *LITTLE* HISTORY

It's generally agreed that runes have been around at least since the 2nd century B.C.E. (although there's some evidence they have been around longer than that). To put that in perspective, that's 800 years before the estimated time that the first tarot cards started to show up! While there is no consensus on exactly where the runes originated, most evidence points to Northern and Western Europe within the Norse and Germanic cultures.

Runes were considered to be aligned with various aspects of life, nature, and magic. People carved runes into their homes to bring prosperity and safety, onto their weapons to assure

successful hunting, into the sides of ships for safe sailing . . .
Basically, runes were carved anyplace people wished to have
help from the gods to make their lives better.

Rune masters were sacred as it was their job to use the runes
to bring rain to the crops, heal those who were sick, and bring
success to warriors. Generally, they were involved in all aspects
of people's lives. In a time when being able to read was a very
rare thing, a rune master was literate in a language that was
considered true magic. He or she could read the runes to get
messages, and this was amazing to the people of the time.

Rune work ebbed and flowed over the centuries, but it never
completely faded away. The runes had a sort of revival in 1983
with the publishing of *The Book of Runes* by Ralph Blum. Mr.
Blum did for runes what I tried to do for tarot—made it accessible to everyone in a way that wasn't fear-based or difficult
to understand. His book is one of my favorites on the topic of
runes, and I really like his approach. However, he doesn't follow
the traditional order of the rune symbols, so if you check out his
book, keep that in mind.

Here's a fun fact: The term *runes* has several ancient literary
meanings, but in general it tends to mean "secrets" or "mysteries." I found that fascinating because, as you may recall, *arcana*
in tarot also means "secrets" or "mysteries."

As I mentioned in Chapter 1, familiarizing yourself with the
history and myths of any particular Divine language can make
a big difference in how it serves you—or sometimes it will make
no difference. In the case of runes, I rather think that the history is somewhat pertinent, whereas the myths are less so. But
here they are in a nutshell.

The myth surrounding runes is related to old Norse gods.
(And, as with most things about these gods, it comes with a
few gory details.) The god Odin was said to have hung himself
from Yggdrasil, otherwise known as the World Tree. He stabbed
himself with his own sword (ick!), and then hung upside down
from the tree for nine days and nights without food or water.
Starving, in pain, and no doubt suffering from a really bad

dehydration headache, the runes presented themselves to him. He then brought them into the world.

Like all myths, there's *way* more to it than that, but that at least gives you an idea.

THE RUNES

Runes are beautifully complex, with a great depth of message and inspiration. Each rune is connected to a letter from the alphabet, a tree, an herb, a Nordic god, and many other elements. Many hefty books have been written about the meanings of each rune and how they interact with one another. Even if I had the space in this compendium to include all of that data, I still would refrain. All that overwhelming information is what kept me from exploring runes for many years. Now that I've discovered how wonderful they are, I want to give you just the basics of each rune in a very simplified manner so that you can get an understanding of them without feeling like you're having to read an encyclopedia.

Keep in mind that working with runes has a lot to do with which rune is sitting next to which other runes. A particular rune's sunny disposition can be completely changed if it is sitting next to a challenging rune, and vice versa. If you discover that runes fascinate you, then learning those combinations will be very important.

Another thing to be aware of is that there are discrepancies in the names of some of the runes. When that is the case, I've tried to use the most common name.

While this is an *extremely* simplified definition of each rune, hopefully it'll give you the basic idea of the general language structure of the Elder Futhark runes. (Please note that the "reversed" meanings refer to when runes are laid and read upside down.)

Freyr's Aett

Fehu: Earned income. Deserved recognition and a sense of fulfillment for what you've worked hard for. Success that is to come, or possible exciting, new opportunities. *Reversed:* The need to make changes in your plans lest there be losses or disappointments. Financial success that fades away and is replaced with frustrating complications.

Uruz: Strength, courage, willpower, good health. Sudden changes that should be embraced. Success that comes with great speed but may require you to adapt and take chances that might make you nervous. Take them anyway! *Reversed:* Unmotivated. Not putting the necessary energy into a situation to be a success. A disappointment or an illness. Be careful!

Thurisaz: Protection. Unexpected good luck often from an unexpected source. Consider other people's opinions. Think things through before acting. *Reversed:* Throwing caution to the wind. Headstrong and not listening to advice, which leads to negative consequences. Luck runs out.

Ansuz: Higher education or tests that you'll easily pass. Wise advice given by caring people that you should seriously heed. The opportunity to learn a new trade from someone kind. *Reversed:* People that can't be trusted. Advice from someone with an ulterior motive. Miscommunication.

Raido: Travel that is safe and purely for fun, often with charming people. A metaphorical journey surrounding life or spirituality. Legal situations are resolved in your favor. A good time to negotiate (but check the fine print). *Reversed:* Challenging travel or travel for unhappy reasons. Relationships that need your attention. Plans that don't go as you'd hoped.

Kenaz: The end of challenging times. New beginnings. Vibrant health or a full recovery from illness. A birth (literal or metaphorical) and creativity. Strength and almost endless energy. *Reversed:* Endings. Relationships that no longer serve and that should be released. Changes that are challenging but that should be embraced.

Gebo: A gift. Financial abundance. Happiness and immense good fortune. A joyful relationship. A happy marriage. *Reversed:* There's no reverse for gebo as it's the same right side up as it is upside down.

Wunjo: Happiness! A very positive solution to your problems. Information that brings great joy. Loving your work. *Reversed:* Troublemakers. Difficulty getting anything accomplished. Unhappy employment. A bad time to sign contracts.

Hagal's Aett

Hagalaz: A loss of power to someone else. Having your plans completely disrupted. Having no control and the anxiety that causes. Fighting the situation causes more grief. A bad time to take risks. *Reversed:* There's no reversed definition for this rune.

Nauthiz: The need to reconsider your plans due to a great risk of failure. The need for patience and restraint. Health issues. Romantic problems. Being a drama queen (or king). *Reversed:* Definitely cancel your plans! Stubbornly moving forward leads to disaster. Wait until conditions are more favorable.

Isa: Putting everything on hold. A cessation of activity. A separation in a business or romantic relationship. An opportunity to look at things differently that you might eventually be grateful for. Can sometimes refer to one year. *Reversed:* There's no reversed definition for Isa.

Jera: Seeds well sown. Your efforts will yield good results. The need for patience. Legal issues or concerns. A warning against gossip or talking about things you don't fully understand. *Reversed:* There's no additional meaning for this rune.

Eihwaz: A delicate situation that requires tact and caution. Small challenges that'll soon resolve themselves. Obstacles or delays that turn out to be beneficial. Impossible problems that turn out okay. *Reversed:* There's no reversed definition for eihwaz.

Pertho: Positive surprises. Hidden information or secrets that get revealed. Heightened psychic abilities. The return of something thought to be gone forever. *Reversed:* The revealing of secrets you were trying to hide. Financial losses. A warning not to gamble or lend money to anyone. Lower your expectations.

Algiz: Help that comes from unanticipated sources. Lots of social activity and new friends. Career opportunities or new studies. Accurate psychic insights that should be heeded. Divine protection. *Reversed:* Self-deception or trickery by others. Vulnerability due to associating with people of low character. Being accused of something you're innocent of.

Sowulo: Victory and success! Good wins over evil. Strong health or the full and swift recovery from an illness. The danger of trying to do too much. *Reversed:* There's no reversed meaning of sowulo.

Tyr's Aett

Teiwaz: Success in all you attempt. Great motivation and the desire to compete or take on a cause. A sign to be fearless in your endeavors. Rapid recovery from injuries or illness. Happiness in romance. *Reversed:* A lack of motivation. Feeling like you just want to give up. Low energy. A relationship that is ending. Infidelity. A lack of creativity.

Berkana: Pregnancy, birth, or the "birth" of new projects or ideas. Your mother, motherhood, or children. Successful pregnancy for those who've been challenged in the past. New beginnings or new romance. *Reversed:* Disagreements and turmoil at home. Receipt of unfortunate news about a member of the family. Fear or worry about someone close to you. Health challenges.

Ehwaz: Positive change. Being on the right path. A relocation or trip. Exciting times. *Reversed:* Sudden or unexpected (though not necessarily bad) changes to your life. Long journeys.

Mannaz: Deserved but overdue success. Assistance from loved ones that should be accepted. The implementation of planned changes. The need to remain modest. Seeking out wise counsel. *Reversed:* Getting in your own way. Going it alone without any assistance from others. Having your plans blocked and your progress impeded. The need to see things from other people's perspective.

Laguz: Divine guidance and protection. Dangers averted by psychic gifts or prophetic dreams. Follow your intuition. Help from others. A positive change in fortune. The end of challenges. *Reversed:* Being tempted to do the wrong thing. Being misled by your intuition. A bad sign. The need to take action immediately. A woman that brings trouble into your life.

Inguz: Successfully completing something challenging. A positive and significant life event. The beginning of a new phase in your life. The impossible becomes possible. The end of stress. *Reversed:* There's no reversed definition for this rune.

Dagaz: A positive and powerful change in your life. Increased abundance and prosperity. A slow and steady path to success. A new beginning. The breaking down of barriers. *Reversed:* There's no reversed meaning for dagaz.

Othila: Material possessions or money. Inheritances or money that comes from investments or retirement. Someone who doesn't mind working hard for what they want. *Reversed:* A bad time to try to buck the system. Delays and actions that go nowhere. Legal disputes. Embarrassing situations.

And finally, the rune that stands outside of any of the aetts . . .

Wyrd: The unknown, undecided, or that which is yet to be resolved. Fate, but fate that might be slightly changed. That which you can't expect to know at this time. A challenge to your faith.

RUNEY TUNES, OR MAKING THE RUNES SING!

Before working with runes, as with all oracles, I recommend that you ask for enlightenment, guidance, and protection by saying a prayer to whatever higher power you like or doing a meditation that focuses on these things. Could be God, the angels, an ascended master, or just simply the Source of All That Is. It was common in ancient times to say a prayer to Odin and Freya, the Norse god and goddess most associated with the runes; you could do that if that feels right to you.

Runes are most often laid out in a spread. Spreads of one, three, and six runes are most common, but there are endless varieties. Here's the structure of those three:

- **One-Rune Spread:** Pull a single rune from the bag. This will shed insight into a situation you're asking about or just what you need to know today.

- **Three-Rune Spread:** Rune one (left) is the challenge, rune two (center) is the suggested action to take, and rune three (right) is the probable outcome if you follow the guidance provided by rune two.

- **Six-Rune Spread (the Runic Cross):** Rune one is the past, rune two is the present, rune three is the immediate future, rune four is the basis of the situation or how you got where you are, rune five refers to obstacles or challenges to come, and rune six is the eventual outcome if no changes are made.

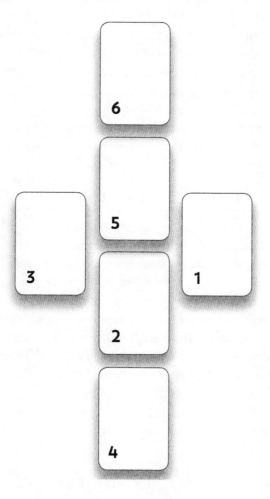

Figure 6.1. Six-rune spread: the Runic Cross

After choosing a spread, think of a question that you seek enlightenment on, and then pull the appropriate number of runes from the bag. Historically, it was customary to place the stones blank side up on a white or colored cloth, but to be honest, I haven't used a cloth and have still gotten amazing insights. The runes are then turned over one by one and read for insight into the query. Some readers of the runes will pull a stone from the bag, write down what the stone was for a position, and then place the stone back into the bag before drawing another rune for the next position. This provides the opportunity for a stone to show up more than once in any reading. (For example, in a three-rune spread, if the same rune shows up for positions one and two, then the challenges currently being experienced are going to continue for a while.)

Runes can be read upside down or "reversed." Or at least, 16 of them can. Eight of the runes are the same right side up as they are upside down and therefore only have one meaning.

MANIFESTING WITH THE RUNES: CARVING OUT YOUR PERFECT FUTURE

A great deal has been written about using runes to manifest your needs and desires—more than could be included in this book. But the easiest methods to apply refer to simply carrying the appropriate rune for your situation with you. You might wear the symbol as a necklace or carry the rune in your pocket. Some people practice drawing the symbol repeatedly over days or weeks until what they're wishing for occurs (or doesn't occur).

It's also common to create a series of runes that are carved in wood or written on paper, or however you wish to "publish" them. Think of it as creating a story. For example, othel and fehu together are great for attracting prosperity and abundance.

THE PERSISTENT PERTHO

I first started buying runes decades ago. I honestly was just buying them because I loved how they looked. They tended to come as beautiful crystals like rose quartz or citrine with gold lettering carved into the stones. They often had a lovely match-ing bag. And let's face it . . . everyone likes their oracle to match their bag!

The truth is, though, I never really worked with them. I would buy a set, leave them out for a while, and then eventually just put them in a drawer. Part of the problem was that when I would start to study runes, I would feel overwhelmed by the history, the myths, and the many possible layers of meaning for each stone. Of course, some of those same things that once filled me with dread now fascinate me. (Although I'm still not that interested in the myths!) But luckily for you, my dear, you have me to boil all of this information down into easy-to-understand chunks. How far you take it is entirely up to you.

I pulled my first rune out of its bag while doing research for this book. I have to say, I was completely blown away! The rune I chose was an upright pertho. And so I grabbed the book that came with the runes to find out what it meant. The thing that really impressed me was that I randomly opened the book to search for the section on pertho, but no searching was nec-essary: I had opened the book to exactly the page that began the discussion of that particular rune. Talk about validation! As detailed earlier in this chapter, pertho represents hidden infor-mation or secrets that get revealed as well as heightened psychic abilities. What was I doing at that moment? Writing this book about ancient oracles whose purpose is to reveal hidden infor-mation and develop intuition!

Two days later, I decided it was time to pull another rune. So I reached down into my little pouch, moved the stones around, and pulled out a rune. Well, color me oh-so-surprised if it wasn't an upright pertho again! This time I decided to use a different book for guidance into the meaning of this rune; once again, I opened this book to the exact page where pertho was explained. I was completely blown away to have that happen a second time! It was then that I truly became a believer in the power of runes. It was as if the runes were telling me, "We know what you're doing!"

THE RAD-SCOOP ON RUNES

The writing of this book brought many exciting revelations for me, and I have to say runes were one of my most pleasant surprises. I love the depth of meaning and the layered nuances they present. I love that they're so easy to carry along wherever I go. I also love that they had so much in familiar with my beloved tarot.

Though, in truth, just a quick check of the time line shows that the proper thing to say is that my beloved tarot has a lot in common with runes.

I found the energy of working with runes to match their ancient history. Their messages can be direct and simple (like my "persistent pertho") or they can be more obscure and require a lot of thought and meditation to understand. I felt that when I asked the runes something simple the answer I would get was also simple—even playful, at times. If I asked the runes something serious, that energy was mirrored back to me with wisdom that felt as though it came from an old mentor or guru. Occasionally those messages seem to say, "Here's a hint. But you'll be richer if you figure the rest out yourself." Either way, the revelations are powerful.

CHAPTER 7

THE MAGIC OF PENDULUMS

ARE PENDULUMS THE RIGHT CHOICE FOR YOU?

- Is an oracle that is very simple to use and easy to learn appealing to you?
- Would you like an oracle that can easily (and discreetly) be carried with you at all times?
- Do you have a desire to consult the Divine on a frequent basis?
- Does having instant access to your subconscious thoughts and motives intrigue you?

As old as runes are, the art of dowsing has been employed by humans for far longer. Dowsing is most often thought of as using two metal rods to seek out water, minerals, and lost items. Pendulums are a version of dowsing that is more often used for getting information or divinatory messages from the Divine via your subconscious.

Many people are familiar with the act of using a pendulum to discover the gender of an unborn baby. This is a sweet use of a pendulum, but it unfairly relegates the art to almost a parlor game, when pendulums are far, far more than that. When mastered, they're a direct line to the wisdom of the Universe and the mysteries of your own subconscious. And mastering the pendulum is actually an easy thing to do.

Pendulums are incredibly easy to use, and almost anything can act as one. You can place a paper clip on the end of a string, or use a wedding band tied to a piece of ribbon, and voilà—you have a pendulum! Store-bought and artisan-created pendulums come in many varieties made of metal, stone, wood, and crystals. Personally, I prefer the crystal types not only because they are so attractive but also because of the manifesting and healing properties that crystals bring to the table.

There is a dizzying array of pendulums to choose from online and in metaphysical bookstores, so you can easily find something that really resonates with you. Some pendulumists (say *that* three times fast!) have many different pendulums, saving certain ones for specific purposes. For example, they might have one for decision-making, one for finding lost items, and a completely different one for spiritual or divinatory insights.

JUST A *LITTLE* HISTORY

Pendulums go way, way back in the history of humankind. There's evidence of the use of pendulums in ancient China, the reign of the pharoahs of Egypt, and the ancient Roman Empire. Their use also moves across many different cultures, including Greek, Hindu, Hebrew, and many more. Curiously, many of the most famous proponents of dowsing were Roman Catholic priests, abbots, and bishops. Stories of leaders of the Roman Catholic Church researching and using dowsing go back as far as the 17th century.

Dowsing and pendulum use really started to gain more and more popularity in the early 20th century, when two abbots brought this science/art to the attention of the public: Abbot Alexis Bouly and Abbot Alexis Mermet. They wrote now-famous books on the topic, stunning the public and even governments with their abilities to find water, missing people, animals, and minerals. Other dowsers started to discover the power of the pendulum for medical purposes, and doctors began to use them in their medical practices.

While all of this shows the immense opportunities provided by the use of a pendulum, our focus is on how to use the pendulum to get answers from the Divine and manifest things you desire in your life. So let's move on!

A LITTLE MOVEMENT GOES A LONG WAY

There are endless theories and speculations about how pendulums work. Fortunately for you, I've done the research, and here's what I believe it all boils down to.

It's my perspective that pendulums are touching the subconscious within all of us—which, in turn, is connected to the Divine. Pendulums draw their answers by going directly through the subconscious, whereas other oracles are more of a mix between a direct path to messages from the Universe and the subconscious. I don't see this route as being better or worse than the other oracles, but it does provide an opportunity for self-understanding that can be very interesting and useful. Working with a pendulum just *feels* different than working with other oracles.

Are people who use pendulums making the pendulum move via tiny, almost imperceptible muscle movements? The vast majority of experts on the subject would tell you the answer to that question is a resounding *yes*. Does that negate the validity or the Divine nature of the information being provided? I would tell you absolutely not!

When we shuffle tarot cards or place our hand into a pouch of runes, we're allowing for the Divine to guide our hands to bring forth the messages or answers we seek. The same is true of working with a pendulum. Our subconscious knows the answer to the questions we ask when it ever so slightly moves the hand that holds the pendulum. The fact that our bodies are moving the pendulum is irrelevant if we have faith that God is always within us and always wants to provide us with the answers we seek.

There are some amazing experts on dowsing that have put together far more scientific explanations for how dowsing and pendulums work. If that is of interest to you, then I would suggest you check out *Dowsing: The Ultimate Guide for the 21st Century* by Elizabeth Brown.

HOLDING YOUR PENDULUM

As I mentioned earlier, just about anything with a little weight tied to the end of a string or ribbon can be used as a pendulum. So you can try out this method of divination without spending anything. But if you'd like to purchase a pendulum of your own, I do recommend it. Find something that feels good to you and resonates with your desire to get answers. It's generally considered best to purchase a pendulum that comes to a point at the end. A point helps you see exactly where the pendulum is drawn to, especially when working with a pendulum chart.

Pendulum charts are drawn on paper. They usually consist of circles or half circles with lines drawn on them to break the circles and semicircles into pieces. (Please see the example in Figure 7.1.) Different words are written within those "pie slices," whether it's different times of the year or options you're trying to choose from. If you truly come to master working with a pendulum, then you might find these charts useful in the future to bring nuance to your readings.

Figure 7.1. Sample pendulum chart

To hold your pendulum, take the tip of the string in your dominant hand, the hand you use most often to write with or pick something up. Place your elbow on a table or any surface, and allow the weight to hang freely from your thumb and index finger. (Please see Figure 7.2.)

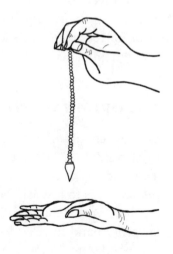

Figure 7.2. Holding a pendulum, method #1

Some people prefer to have several inches of the chain of the pendulum fully in their palm, allowing the chain to drape across the top of their hand, over their index finger, so that the weight hangs freely, as in Figure 7.3.

Figure 7.3. Holding a pendulum, method #2

The pendulum should feel comfortable in your hand, and the weight should hang down about 5 inches from your fingers. However, if a shorter or longer length feels better to you, then, as always, follow your own guidance.

PENDULUMS: THE ORIGINAL SWINGERS!

To begin working with pendulums, we're going to start by figuring out the options of "yes," "no," "I don't know," and "answer not available." You can discover or program your pendulum for these answers. My preference is to just ask the pendulum.

The first step is to hold your pendulum in one hand, completely still. Use your other hand to cease its movement if you need to. Then ask your pendulum, "Show me yes," and watch to see what movement it makes.

The most common movements are:

- a straight line moving back and forth, left to right
- a straight line moving away from your body then back to your body
- a circle moving clockwise
- a circle moving counterclockwise
- not moving at all

Take your time. The pendulum might move immediately or it might take a few minutes—or even a few tries. Any movement might seem very slow or slight at first, but it'll become more significant as you wait.

Once you've established what yes looks like for your pendulum, bring it to a complete stop again. Now ask, "Show me no." Usually no is the opposite movement from yes—for example, a clockwise circle rather than a counterclockwise circle. But nothing is outside possibility. If yes is a straight line left to right for you but no is a clockwise circle, just go with it.

Follow the same method to find out your pendulum's movements for "I don't know" and "answer not available." Sometimes the pendulum will have its own ideas for these answers. For me, "yes" is the pendulum swinging in a straight line from left to right, "no" is the pendulum swinging in a straight line away from and then back to my body, "I don't know" is a counterclockwise circle, and "answer not available" is the pendulum simply refusing to move at all.

An alternative method to asking the pendulum is *telling* it what its movements should be. I think it's a more natural method to let the pendulum tell you, but if you've strong feelings about this, go ahead and program it. If you want yes to be a clockwise motion, then say to your pendulum, "This is yes," and move it in a clockwise circle. If no is counterclockwise, then make the movement while telling the pendulum, "This is no."

In my research, I was a little surprised to discover that the motions your pendulum presents for yes, no, and all the rest can change from session to session! Therefore, it's probably a good idea to test a pendulum for the answers before each day's use. After I discovered this possibility, I did a quick check of my pendulum, and the motions for the answers hadn't changed. But it's always best to be sure!

YES, NO, MAYBE SO

Yes and no as answers are pretty self-explanatory. But let's talk about "I don't know" and "answer not available."

Why would an oracle tell you "I don't know"? In my experience, that usually reflects a poorly worded question. For example, if you ask the pendulum if you should move to Chicago or Los Angeles, your pendulum won't be able to answer that because it's not a "yes or no" question; it's an "or" question.

Pendulum work is about breaking things down into small, specific pieces. Frankly, I find the Universe as a whole to be a very literal place that requires very specific questions to get accurate answers.

Going back to our example, you should first ask the pendulum, "Should I move to Chicago?" After getting your answer, *then* ask it, "Should I move to Los Angeles?" If both places are of interest to you, then be sure to ask about both cities, even if the answer to the first city you mentioned is yes. It's totally possible that both cities will have an answer of yes, indicating that either city would make you happy.

Pay attention to how enthusiastically the pendulum swings or moves for each city. The more dramatic the answer, the happier you're likely to be in that city. If the movements are the same, then it's probably time to ask more questions. You can ask things like "Would I be financially successful in Chicago?" or "Would I find true love in Los Angeles?"

Poorly worded questions can also get you inaccurate answers with a pendulum. This is usually because you didn't really think the question through thoroughly. Let's go back to our moving question. Let's pretend you've got Atlanta on your mind, and you're really thinking about moving. You ask the pendulum, "Should I move?" It says yes, so you pack your bags and move to Atlanta, but it's not at all what you'd hoped for. What went wrong?

Consider that you asked a very broad question with "Should I move?" Your pendulum said yes because you really need to move to a house with a more positive energy—but in the same city you're living in. Should you move? Yes! To Atlanta? Well, you didn't ask that, did you?

Now, why would you get "answer not available"? I've actually experienced this answer with angel work and tarot cards sometimes. Source knows the path to your happiness far better than you do. Sometimes having a particular piece of information before you're ready for it could really trip you up. It's tempting to be alarmed by this answer, but you shouldn't be. You should just trust that the answers you seek will be revealed in perfect timing.

Pendulums, like other oracles, aren't toys. However, unlike other oracles, pendulums tend to be treated as such. It's really not a good idea to ask your pendulum pointless or senseless questions. By doing so, you're telling both your subconscious and the Universe that you're not taking the connection seriously. However, this isn't the same as asking your pendulum questions for training purposes.

For example, as a beginner it's perfectly fine to ask your pendulum "Am I breathing?" to test whether you have the yes and no movements correct. As you practice, you might ask your pendulum "Are my keys in the kitchen?" even if you know full well that they are. This is just learning the pendulum and becoming more in tune with it. However, it's not a good idea to ask your pendulum "Should I wear the blue shirt or the red shirt today?" just to play around with it.

Speaking of your keys, one of the perfectly acceptable uses for your pendulum is to locate lost items. You can ask a series of questions that lead you to what you're trying to locate. In this example, you might start with "Are my car keys in the house?"

(Remember to be specific about what keys you're looking for if you own more than one set.) If you get a yes, then you can go room by room asking the pendulum, "Are the car keys in this room?" Or you can just sit somewhere and ask, "Are the car keys in the kitchen?" Once you've narrowed it down to a particular room, you can then ask the pendulum, "Are the car keys near the east wall?"

Once you've become really good at working with your pendulum, you'll be able to track down anything that's become lost so long as it's findable. If you accidentally dropped your keys down a storm drain, then you're probably not getting those back. Though if you're suspicious that could've happened, you could certainly get validation from your pendulum and save yourself the time and trouble of searching for something that's not retrievable.

MANIFESTING WITH THE PENDULUM: SPINNING UP THE MAGIC

There are several ways to use pendulums to manifest your desires. Most of them work via the Law of Attraction by using the pendulum's natural connection with the subconscious to bring it into alignment with your conscious desires. When the conscious and the subconscious are in agreement in a positive way about what you want to create in your life, magic can happen pretty quickly!

One way to manifest with the pendulum is to focus on whatever it is you want to bring into (or remove from) your life. Begin with the normal preparation work for your pendulum. Think about what it is that you're wanting to bring into your life, and then ask the pendulum whether you're currently in an energetic space to make that happen. The pendulum will let you know if you are. If it says yes, then let the pendulum swing in the yes motion while you think joyfully and optimistically about what you want to create. If it says no, then start asking your pendulum what sort of changes you need to make in order to bring about the desired outcome.

In Chapter 1, I told you about the power of energetic connections in our lives and the importance of making sure that they stay clean. Your pendulum can help you clear out any negative energy patterns while at the same time bringing in new things that you want to manifest.

To use this method, after your regular prep work, take your pendulum and start to twirl in a circle it in the counterclockwise direction. While you're doing that, say to yourself, *I now remove all negative energy from my life. All unhealthy or undesired connections with other people are cleared away. My negative thinking is erased. All harmful energetic attachments to others are removed.* While you'll have started the pendulum's movement in the counterclockwise direction, as you say these things, the pendulum will take over. You'll no longer be moving it; you'll just let it spin until it's done.

Depending on how much energy there is to clear, your pendulum might swing pretty wildly, but it'll eventually stop. You'll probably feel lighter, happier, and filled with more energy after this exercise. But consider this: the work you've done has now cleared out a lot of energy that was taking up space in the magical, manifesting machine that lives within you. So now it's time to fill up that space! Otherwise, it'll be easy for negative energy to just rush back in.

Start your pendulum spinning in a circle in a clockwise direction. While it spins, start telling the pendulum what you want to manifest. For example, this might be "I am healthy and strong in all ways, and I am full of energy and motivation to complete all the things I desire to accomplish." Or perhaps you might say, "I am deserving of love. Romance that is supportive and kind finds its way easily into my life." Whatever you're wanting to manifest, make it an affirmation.

The pendulum will once again take over the movement. When it comes to a stop, you'll know that you've filled your magical, manifesting machine all the way up! The more you do this routine, the more quickly things will manifest in your life.

THE HOTLINE!

Priti Mistry says her crystal pendulum is her "BFF across life-times." She considers it to be her connection to her higher self and spiritual team—"her hotline."

I asked Priti about her experiences, and this is what she told me:

> I use the pendulum for almost everything. I've also found a way to check energy compatibility between people, between spaces and people, between companies or institutions and people, and the like. I've been helping friends, family, and clients with this skill.
>
> This is the story of one of my close friends. Her teenage daughter was going through a tough time in her current school. As a mother, she was concerned because her daughter was unhappy and losing interest even in her favorite activities. She's always been a bright kid, outgoing and excellent in her studies. So my client was looking at changing the school, and she sent me a list to check the energy compatibility of each school with her daughter's energy.
>
> I asked my pendulum to rate the energy match of each school on a scale of 1 to 10 with 1 being lowest and 10 being a perfect fit. (I personally go with 10/10 only!) One school fit the bill.
>
> My friend pursued that school and got her daughter admitted there. It's been two years now, and it's wonderful to see her progress in all spheres, be it academics, sports, or any other. She is in grade 10 now, and I got to know that she's been chosen the school captain. How wonderful!
>
> Now that's what I call a perfect fit! When we're in an energetically compatible space, we grow and blossom with love and joy. It feels like home. It's like finding the perfect fit, rather than trying to fit in.

THE RAD-SCOOP ON PENDULUMS

Of all the oracles in this compendium, pendulums might be the easiest to use, especially for quick and impromptu answers. You can easily carry one with you everywhere you go, and so long as you can find a private space (or at least don't mind if you get weird looks from others), you can just pull it out and get super fast yes or no answers. It can help you make decisions—though it might require a lot of yes or no questions to get there—and help you find lost items.

I was impressed and amazed by the pendulum's connection to the subconscious. I could literally feel the connection and thought it was a magical thing to sense one's own inner workings through the pendulum.

I consider the pendulum to be a great addition to my oracle toolbox.

CHAPTER 8

THE MAGIC OF THE I CHING

IS THE I CHING THE RIGHT CHOICE FOR YOU?

- Are you seeking deep insights that make you think?
- Do you tend to perceive all of life's questions as having a spiritual basis?
- Is an oracle that empowers you to be in control of your life and rejects the idea that anything is "fated" appealing to you?

As always, I'm going to be completely honest with you. Studying the I Ching (pronounced "ee cheeng") gave me a colossal headache. But wait! Don't turn away yet. The challenge with the I Ching is that it's full of a lot of different terms and steps. I can truthfully tell you that I had to read four books before I could really grasp the way the I Ching works in order to make it easier to understand. I think I did it, so no headache for you! But let's back up and start with the question "What exactly is the I Ching?"

The I Ching (aka the Book of Changes or the Book of Change) is an ancient Chinese holy book. It's a book of divination, but it's also a book of answers to any question you want to ask it. As with any divination tool, the way you ask the question matters; if the question is not well thought out, you'll get gobbledygook for an answer.

The I Ching is a system based on 64 hexagrams. Hexagrams are six stacked lines—some of which are solid and some of which are broken into two pieces. Here's an example:

Figure 8.1. Hexagram 22, pi (grace)

The lines are created and read from the bottom up, and each line is given a numerical value of 6, 7, 8, or 9. If the line is associated with 7 or 8, then that line is considered to be stable and unchanging. If it's 6 or 9, then that line is in movement.

The I Ching is, after all, the book of change. The divinatory advice it provides isn't just insight into where you are at this moment, but a spiritual barometer of which way the wind is blowing. It tells you what change is coming and what type of change it is. It also gives insight into your part in whatever question you've asked it.

Once you've figured out which hexagram answers your question (I'll explain how that happens later in the chapter), you turn to the page in the book that talks about that particular hexagram and read what insights it has for you. Usually, a hexagram will lead you to a second hexagram, so you'll read that page as well. The answer you receive might make sense right away—and if it does, you have my greatest admiration. However, the most likely scenario (especially for a beginner) is that you'll think you did it wrong. You didn't. Like I said before, the I Ching makes you ponder, and in the pondering, great insights can come.

JUST A *LITTLE* HISTORY

The I Ching goes back 3,000 years or so. Like many other holy books, it was written by several people over a period of years: Fu Xi, King Wen, Wen's son the Duke of Zhou, and Confucius (yes, *that* Confucius).

Originally, the I Ching wasn't made up of hexagrams (figures of six lines) at all. It consisted of eight trigrams (figures of three lines) brought to us by Fu Xi. Later, King Wen combined the eight trigrams to create 64 unique hexagrams of possible messages. He created what were called judgments (or sometimes decisions) for each one that more or less told you whether things looked favorable or not. His son Duke Wen later added meanings for each line. These things helped make the I Ching easier to understand, but it was still confusing. That's when Confucius got involved. He became fascinated with the I Ching and wrote commentaries on each hexagram to explain in more detail what they meant.

Over the millennia, and in the turbulence that was China's government (as well as its competitive mystical communities), the I Ching went in and out of hiding like a groundhog. Now you see it—now you don't. Eventually, in the early 1900s, various scholars became fascinated with it, bringing it back to the attention of the general public.

If you're interested in all the complex history and the story behind the I Ching, there are many books written by college professors that are a strain on the eyes and the brain to read. Some Chinese scholars disagree with the books written by American or European authors as having been "Westernized," so if you're keen on the details, you might want to keep that in mind when choosing authors.

A PATH MADE BY MILLIONS

As I mentioned in Chapter 1, oracles work because people worked with them and believed in them. The I Ching is one of the oldest of all the oracles, so the pathways through the metaphorical forest are well worn. It also has a connection to our subconscious (much like runes) that comes from the pondering of the words.

FIRST THERE WAS ASPIRIN, THEN THERE WAS CLARITY

As I mentioned earlier, fully grasping how to work with the I Ching was a little challenging at first. There are lots of terms for specific aspects of the I Ching that seem almost designed to confuse you. To me, it was a little like reading "To get an answer from the I Ching, you must first boozle the geegles. After the geegles are set in place by the konglebu, you can then use three coins [Oh yay! I can understand three coins!] to create the lederhosen [I'm sorry—what?] that'll lead you to the first caygle to provide your answer."

I'm not kidding. It's like that.

So what I'm going to do now in this rundown is probably infuriate a bunch of I Ching experts by explaining this to you in as simple a way as I can. Please believe me when I honestly say with all my heart that in the end, I found the I Ching amazing and worthy of study. It's not for everyone, but it's worth a try. Okay. Here we go.

The I Ching is made up of 64 hexagrams, which are sets of 6 lines that lead you to the judgments, or commentaries, on those hexagrams. (It's like looking up a guidebook entry when pulling a tarot or oracle card.) Each hexagram represents a symbol that has a name. The symbol has a meaning, but don't worry about that now. You can learn that later if you want, but you don't need to know what the symbols mean to get answers from the I Ching. (Also, there's disagreement about the names attributed to each symbol; don't worry about that either.) All you need to care about is what page each hexagram leads you to and what the message there is.

First, think of a question and write it down. When forming your question, remember that the I Ching doesn't lend itself to "or" or "and" questions very well. So don't ask the I Ching, "Should I move to Chicago or Los Angeles?" And don't ask the I Ching, "Should I take this new job, and will it make me rich?" In fact, the I Ching probably shouldn't be your go-to oracle for extremely simple or routine questions. A question like "Should I go on a date with Bobby?" is probably better answered by a pendulum or an oracle card. The I Ching is good for open-ended questions on weighty matters, like getting insight into life changes or big challenges currently happening to you.

Next, you'll be creating your own hexagram. This used to be done in a complicated way with sticks called yarrow stalks. It was very complex and took half an hour to create just one hexagram—but we can do better than that.

First off, you'll need three identical coins: three pennies, or three nickels, or three of whatever your coinage is. The side of the coin with a face (often called heads) will equal a value of 3. The back of the coin (or the side often called tails) equals a value of 2.

Now pick up the three coins, shake them in your hands, and let them fall onto whatever surface you're using. Add up the value of the coins. If you see two heads and one tail, then that's 3 + 3 + 2 = 8. This is the first line of your hexagram.

Don't like math? I've gotcha covered!

- Three tails = 6
- Two tails and one head = 7
- Two heads and one tail = 8
- Three heads = 9

Those are the only option: 6, 7, 8, and 9. When building your hexagram, here's how those numbers translate:

- 6 and 8 are a broken line, like this: _____   _____
- 7 and 9 are a single solid line, like this: _____

Keep using the three coins like dice. Rattle them about in your hands and drop them a total of six times, each time noting the line type and the number. Make sure you write it down. Also remember that hexagrams are created from the bottom up!

When you're done with your first hexagram, you should have something like this:

(Line 6) _____ 9
(Line 5) _____   _____ 8
(Line 4) _____   _____ 6
(Line 3) _____ 7
(Line 2) _____   _____ 8
(Line 1) _____ 7

Now that you have your hexagram, let's talk about what those numbers mean. I told you that the I Ching is about where you are, changes that are coming, and what your part in all of it is. The numbers 7 and 8 represent no change. But 6 and 9 show that movement is happening. For each hexagram, there's a general message, but there's also a specific message for each *moving* line. After reading the general message for the hexagram, you then read the messages for the lines with a value of 6 or 9. In our hexagram example, that would be the fourth and sixth lines.

All I Ching books have a chart to show what hexagram you've created. The top trigram (top three lines) is listed at the top of the chart, and the lower trigram (the bottom three lines) is shown along the side. Match the top trigram and the bottom one to identify which hexagram you just created. Figure 8.2 shows what they usually look like.

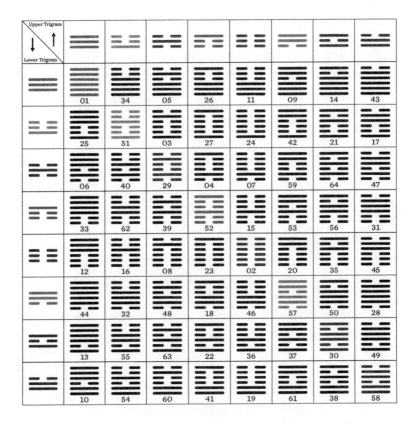

Figure 8.2. Hexagram chart

A quick look at the chart in Figure 8.2 shows that the hexagram created in the example is #22, pi (grace). So you would turn to that page, read the general overall message, and the specific messages for the lines that show movement. The overall message is your situation right now. The movement lines show where changes are happening.

Okay. The next part gets a little tricky. But I'll try to make it as easy as I can.

You're now going to modify the hexagram that you created to reflect the changes that are happening. This is the second hexagram for your reading, which represents your part in what's going on.

For every line with a value of 9, you're going to change the solid line to be a broken line. For every line with a value of 6, you'll change the broken line to be a solid line. For the above example, the hexagram would be changed to this:

(Line 6) ____ ____ 9
(Line 5) ____ ____ 8
(Line 4) _____ 6
(Line 3) _____ 7
(Line 2) ____ ____ 8
(Line 1) _____ 7

A quick look at the chart in Figure 8.2 identifies this second hexagram as #55, feng (abundance). You would then turn to the page about that hexagram and read the general message, but not any of the line messages. Just the general message.

I know that seems like a lot to take in, but now that I've explained it in detail, let's summarize the steps:

- Think of a question. Write it down.

- To find the value for each of the six lines of your hexagram, use three coins like you would dice. Throw the coins six times, noting the value of each line (heads = 3, tails = 2). The only possible outcomes are 6, 7, 8, and 9.

- Draw your hexagram from the bottom up, remembering that lines with a value of 6 or 8 are broken, and lines with a value of 7 or 9 are solid.

- Look at the chart to see which hexagram you created.

- Go to the page where that hexagram is listed and read the overall message.

- Read the message for any line that had the value of 6 or 9.

- Now create your second hexagram. For every 6 in the hexagram, change the broken line to a solid line. For every 9 in the hexagram, change the solid line to a broken line.

- Consult the chart to see what new hexagram you created.

- Go to the page listed and read the overall message (but no line messages).

- Ponder, ponder, ponder the messages from the I Ching until they make sense.

That's as simple as I know how to make it. And once you've done it a couple of times, it does become easier and easier to follow.

If your message doesn't make sense to you, just let it rest. Don't start over and ask the same question to see what different answer you get. I promise that, just as with other oracles, that's going to confuse you. The I Ching is an oracle of patience. The answer will come to you if you let it.

MANIFESTING WITH THE I CHING: IT-CHING TO SUCCEED

Manifesting with the I Ching is about getting answers. You can ask it "What's blocking my heart's desire?" and you'll get deep and enlightening information. You can ask the I Ching how to heal emotional wounds that keep romance at bay or what's causing an illness from a spiritual and subconscious level. The I Ching can help you make changes in your life—and frankly, who you are—so that the things you're wanting to manifest can come to you through the Law of Attraction.

I CHING, RUNES, AND ANGEL NUMBERS (OH MY!)

If you read Chapter 6, "The Magic of Runes," then you recall that I drew a rune from the pouch and then just magically opened the book to the exact same rune. Two days later, I pulled another rune; it was the same rune I pulled before. When I reached for a totally different book on runes, I again opened the book right to the exact page I needed! This was impressive to me.

In doing my first reading with the I Ching, I was equally impressed. I created the hexagram, and then went to look for the corresponding page. What amazed me was that the message of the hexagram was *the same message* I'd just gotten twice from the runes. I was so blown away, I had to call a friend to talk to her about getting the same message three times from two different oracles, over five days!

Later in that same week, I had an energy clearing with an amazing healer. She had brilliant things to say during our time together. After it was over, I decided to ask the I Ching, "What was the most important thing that I learned from this healing session?"

I started tossing pennies, and I was amazed even before I read the message associated with the hexagram. The hexagram came up with 7777 in the middle of the numbers. 7777 in angel numerology means you're on the right spiritual path. In total, the numbers directed me to hexagram 44. As you may recall from the angel chapter, 44 means "the angels are with you." Both of these are things that the energy healer had told me! When I read hexagram 44, it also matched one of the energy healer's main points.

I am a true believer in the I Ching!

THE RAD-SCOOP ON THE I CHING

The I Ching sees all things as having a spiritual aspect. If you ask the I Ching, "Should I take this job?" it'll give you a very definite answer. But it'll also make you think (and think and think) about the part of that question and the situation you now find yourself in that has to do with the Universe as a whole.

To me, there's no doubt that the I Ching is a thinking person's oracle. It isn't about yes or no. A pendulum will give you simple yes or no answers if that's what you're seeking. With the I Ching, it's about yes and *why*. It's about no and *why not*.

I've been 100 percent honest with you that I found the I Ching complicated and challenging to get my head around. Part of that is possibly because I was reading scholarly books on the topic rather than a sort of *I Ching for Dummies*. In researching oracles, I like to understand things at a deeper level so that I can explain them to others in a simpler way. There's *so much more* to the I Ching than I've explained to you in this book. But to explain it all would make this chapter a book of its own.

Now that I understand how to use the I Ching, I'm truly impressed. For deeper issues or more important questions, I'm sure I'll turn to it for answers. Would I turn to the I Ching for simple questions or quick answers? No, I really don't think I would.

If divinatory work is something you're interested in for deep and spiritual reasons, you'll love the I Ching. If you want answers to questions that'll bring about deep inner understanding and perhaps days of revelations, the I Ching will make you positively giddy.

If those things do not inspire you, then it might give you a headache.

CHAPTER 9

THE MAGIC OF ASTROLOGY

IS ASTROLOGY THE RIGHT CHOICE FOR YOU?

- Are you spiritual but with a very logical mind?
- Do you like science?
- Do you find it hard to tap into your intuition but still want guidance?
- Are you interested in what the future holds?

Are you a Leo or Aquarius or Pisces? Virtually everyone has heard of astrology. I've never met a person who didn't at least know "their sign." That being said, astrology is complicated. There are many moving parts to it (literally), and it does take study to get a handle on this mystical science. Most astrologers I know are quite intuitive, but they rely mostly upon the systematic dance of the planets and the stars to get their information. However, just in case you only recently arrived from another planet—pun intended—let me give you the rundown here.

Astrology is a science that involves gathering information about people and their nature based upon where the sun, moon, and planets were at the time of their birth. Predictions can then be done by comparing that birth information to where the planets are in the present and where those celestial bodies will be in the future. And when we say "where," we mean more where they *appear* to be from planet Earth rather than where they *actually* are. Mars may appear to be right next to Saturn in the nighttime sky, but in reality they never get anywhere near one another.

Astrologers take the date, place, and (hopefully) exact time of your birth and place it on a circular chart cut into 12 pielike pieces. That chart represents where the sun, moon, and planets were when you were born. Each one of those 12 pieces represents an aspect of human life. Which planets fall into each of those 12 pieces tells an astrologer something important about how you handle love, career, relationships with your family, money, and much more. I'll show you how those pieces come together later in this chapter.

As I said, astrology is complex, but it's also pretty amazing! Many people through the millennia have discovered a great love for it, and I personally adore it, but I don't consider myself an expert. I do understand all the pieces and parts, and I can look at someone's astrological chart and make some basic interpretations. However, if I want astrological information, I go to a professional. I have an annual "checkup" with my astrologer every year, and I would never begin something very important without checking in with her first.

In this chapter, I'm going to help you understand the basics in terms that are as simple as possible. But as with all of the oracles in this compendium, there's way more to astrology than the tiny taste I'm giving you here. Countless books have been written about astrology for thousands of years. Should you catch the "astrology bug," you'll have no lack of reading material to choose from.

JUST A *LITTLE* HISTORY

I told you astrology is complex. It's also old, old, *old*! It's pretty easy to trace astrology back 4,000 years. Most people believe it's far older than that, but the history has gotten lost. The Babylonians, Mesopotamians, Egyptians, and Mayans all had their versions of astrology. As Alexander the Great tromped throughout Asia, the Greeks learned the ways of many foreign cultures and couldn't help but be influenced by what they learned. Information from the Sumerians and Chaldeans about astrology began to influence how the Greeks saw the stars.

You have to keep in mind that, back then, astrology and astronomy were basically considered to be the same thing. Astrologers were generally astronomers and vice versa. In the 2nd century C.E., a Greco-Roman mathematician, astronomer, geographer, and astrologer named Claudius Ptolemy was watching the planets' movements with great precision. It was his work that shaped astrology into the form it basically still exists in today.

That isn't to say that astronomy has remained completely the same since Ptolemy. Uranus and Neptune weren't even discovered until 1781 and 1846 respectively. Pluto wasn't found until 1930. Ceres, a dwarf planet between Saturn and Uranus that you've probably never even heard of, was uncovered in 1977. Ceres is less than half the size of Pluto, yet astrologers have determined that it has a significant part to play in astrology.

As of this writing, there's a growing debate among *astronomers* as to whether we're missing a planet. I'm not talking about that silly story that flies around the Internet every couple of years about some fictional planet that is going to crash into Earth. I'm talking about serious astronomy.

Scientists have noticed that objects in the farthest reaches of our solar system are behaving strangely—as though they are being thrown around by the gravitational pull of an unseen world. This unseen planet has been estimated to be four times as large as Earth and ten times as massive. When scientists placed Planet Nine, the nickname for this world, into their mathematical models, suddenly the behavior of the erratic objects in the outer solar system made perfect sense.

The only reason I'm telling you about Planet Nine is that should it be discovered, *astrologers* would then have to reassess their science and determine how Planet Nine fits into astrology. They had to do those same types of reassessments when Uranus, Neptune, Pluto, and Ceres were discovered. So while astrology is fairly well set in the 21st century, new discoveries could still bring big changes to the practice.

THE GRAVITY OF THE SITUATION

We can look at astrology as being a well-worn path through a spiritual forest. It works because for thousands of years people have believed it works. However, there are other possible explanations.

First, some astrologers believe that you chose the date, time, and place of your birth before you came into this lifetime. This was done so that the energy of the planets would be a good match for what you were coming to earth to learn. Therefore astrology is, in its own way, a sort of reverse engineering to interpret what you were wanting to learn by seeing what energies were in play at the time of your birth.

Second, each of the celestial bodies in astrology has a gravitational pull. There's more about gravity that scientists *don't* know than they *do* know. Some astrologers believe that subtle gravitational waves also make waves in our lives.

Finally, as we learn more and more about the science of quantum physics, scientists are having to give more and more credence to concepts like the Law of Attraction. Quantum particles act like waves until they're observed. It's as if they're pushed into particle form by the very action of looking at them! Today's astrologers are monitoring discoveries in quantum physics closely as a possible way to link the science of astrology to more mainstream science.

STARS IN YOUR EYES

All right, everyone! Astrology class is now in session. In this section, I'm going to give you the most basic pieces of astrology. Remember, there's far, far more to it than I'm explaining to you in this chapter. However, this should give you a basic understanding so that you can decide if astrology is the language of the Divine for you.

When most people think of astrology, they only think about being an Aries—or a Gemini, or whatever sign they were born under. Technically, the zodiac sign that most people know about is called your "sun sign." Astrology, however, is far more three-dimensional than that. Saying that you know exactly who someone is because you know that their sun sign is Capricorn is like saying you know exactly who someone is because his eyes are green or her hair is blonde. Suggesting that two people aren't romantically compatible because one is a Leo and the other is a Pisces is equally oversimplifying. Let me show you why . . .

In astrology, the sky is split up into the 12 sections of the zodiac. As the Earth spins, the sun, the moon, and the planets all move through those different zodiac signs or sections. The closer a planet is to Earth, the faster it moves through all 12 signs. For example, our moon zips through all 12 signs in 28 days, staying in each sign for about 2 to 2½ days. Mars takes about 2 years to go through all the signs. Jupiter takes approximately 12 years to tiptoe through the zodiac. The sun spends about 30 days or so in each sign, as the zodiac has 12 signs and there are 12 months in a year.

Each of these 12 zodiac sections is called a house, and each house represents a different part of your life. These 12 houses are the foundation upon which astrology is built. Think of it like a skeleton. A skeleton doesn't make a body; it's just the structure that a body is built upon. Without a brain, a heart, muscles, eyes, a face, and so on, the body is not complete. Here is what the 12 houses represent:

- **First House:** Personality, appearance, how you see yourself, how you portray yourself to others, beginnings, your general outlook on life

- **Second House:** Sense of self-worth, self-esteem, material possessions, how you spend and treat money, daily routines

- **Third House:** Communication, intellect, childhood, early education, siblings, local travel, neighborhoods, relatives other than parents, and messages

- **Fourth House:** Home (both birth and current), family, your upbringing, early foundations, the caregiver in the household, most astrologers say mothers (but some say fathers), land, and ancestry

- **Fifth House:** Love and romance (including affairs), children, having fun, gambling, creativity, risk taking, and entertainment

- **Sixth House:** Health, fitness, exercise, daily work, service to others, caretaking, pets, daily routines, activities, and jobs

- **Seventh House:** Marriage, confidants, partners in work or relationships, enemies, contracts, legal issues, separation, and divorce

- **Eighth House:** Death and rebirth, sex, things you own with your spouse or other people, other people's money, taxes, inheritance, psychic abilities, and taboo subjects

- **Ninth House:** Spirituality, learning, teaching, higher education, long-distance travel, knowledge, books, publishing, morality, ethics, religion, inspiration, optimism, and high ideals

- **Tenth House:** Career, corporations, fame, public image, status, reputation, most astrologers say fathers (but some say mothers), government, authority, and ambitions

- **Eleventh House:** Friendships, groups, clubs, like-minded people, social justice, society, humanitarian causes, hopes and dreams

- **Twelfth House:** Mysteries, mysticism, things that are hidden from us, the unconscious, the subconscious, endings, old age, secret relationships, hospitals, prison, methods of confinement, unknown enemies

The next thing you need to know is that each house is "ruled" by a sign of the zodiac. It's what gives the house its energy. This is awesome, as I can share with you the sign of each house while also telling you about the energy that each sign of the zodiac feels like.

Just like people, all the signs have upsides and downsides. Healthy people exhibit the positive traits in the following list. Unhealthy, stressed, or distressed people may display the negative traits. Each sign of the zodiac also has a symbol, called a glyph, and an associated planet.

First House, Aries: Adventurous, courageous, self-starter, energetic, confident, leadership, optimistic, ambitious, hot-tempered, and aggressive; associated with the planet Mars

Second House, Taurus: Patient, persistent, determined, grounded, sensual, affectionate, dependable, romantic, stubborn, and sometimes self-centered; associated with the planet Venus

Third House, Gemini: Intellectual, chatty, witty, adaptable, curious, sometimes nosy, always thinking, can be inconsistent or even superficial; associated with the planet Mercury

Fourth House, Cancer: Loving, compassionate, emotional, intuitive, family focused, cautious, imaginative, moody, dramatic, and can be dishonest; associated with the moon

Fifth House, Leo: Warm, enthusiastic, magnetic, generous, faithful, loving, creative, arrogant, and bossy; associated with the sun

Sixth House, Virgo: Caretaker, reliable, practical, perfectionist, intelligent, analytical, helpful, picky, critical, and a worrier; associated with Mercury

Seventh House, Libra: Harmonious, impartial, charming, diplomatic, romantic, attractive, idealistic, tactful, indecisive, and conflict averse; associated with the planet Venus

Eighth House, Scorpio: Powerful, passionate, sexual, extremely loyal, intuitive, heroic, jealous, vengeful, and unforgiving; associated with the planet Pluto

Ninth House, Sagittarius: Optimistic (sometimes blindly so) funny, happy, spiritual, honest, enthusiastic, generous, inspiring, loyal, blunt, restless, and fickle; associated with the planet Jupiter

Tenth House, Capricorn: Practical, disciplined, determined, ambitious, tireless, cautious, diplomatic, selfish, and prideful; associated with the planet Saturn

Eleventh House, Aquarius: Brilliant, honest, original, loyal, humanitarian, innovative, rebellious, inflexible, and closed-minded; associated with the planet Uranus

Twelfth House, Pisces: Sensitive, intuitive, kind, selfless, gentle, shy, prone to depression, unconfident, and weak willed; associated with the planet Neptune

Whew! So now you've got some of the basic pieces. These 12 signs encompass intellect, heart, passions, and even physical traits. Think of the energies of the planets, zodiac signs, and the houses as being the spiritual DNA that makes you the fascinating, complex, and unique person that you are! Now you have something to hang on that skeleton otherwise known as an astrological chart.

CREATING YOUR ASTROLOGICAL CHART

An astrological chart is a snapshot of where the sun, moon, and planets are in any given moment. The planets are constantly dancing with one another. The sky is always changing. So you can look at a chart for any time in the past, the present, or the future! Figure 9.1 shows what a blank astrological chart looks like. (For a closer look at the astrological charts in this chapter, please visit www.radleighvalentine.com/compendium.)

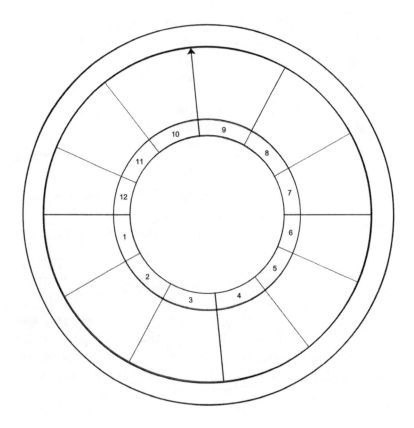

Figure 9.1. A blank astrological chart

A birth chart is an astrological chart for the moment you were born. Most astrologers consider the three most important aspects of a chart to be your sun, moon, and rising signs. (I also consider the north and south nodes to be very important, but let's save that for later.) It's all very simple. Your sun sign is the sign of the zodiac where the sun was when you were born. Your moon sign is the sign that the moon occupied at the time of your birth. Finally, your rising sign (also known as the ascendant) is the zodiac sign that was on the eastern horizon at the moment of your birth—and this information orients your chart. (Do you understand now why the *exact* time of your birth for that snapshot is pretty important?)

Because the zodiac signs change quickly throughout the day, determining which sign each house is in is very tricky. In fact, it's rather like a revolving wheel of fortune. Perhaps you've watched the television game show *Wheel of Fortune* or played a game at a carnival or fair where a big wheel split into pie pieces (rather like an astrological chart) spins round and round. Where the wheel stops tells you what you won or, more likely, didn't win.

I once had a dear friend tell me he had been born at 2:02 P.M. The next day, he told me that he'd made a mistake; he had actually been born at 2:20 P.M. Those mere 18 minutes completely changed which astrological sign each house of his chart was in! While exact timing is very important, if you don't have an exact time, a professional astrologer may be able to make a very educated guess.

Now it's time to show you some examples. We're going to go slow, because I think showing you a complete chart if you know nothing about astrology might blow your brain. So one little piece at a time.

Let's say that you were born on June 12, 1972, in San Diego, California, at 4:44 P.M. That'd mean that Scorpio was on the eastern horizon at the moment of your birth, making Scorpio your rising sign. June 12 is a Gemini date, so your sun is in Gemini. This would be expressed as "You're Gemini with Scorpio rising."

If Aries had been on the horizon at the time of your birth, then you would be Aries rising. It would also mean that the first house would be in its natural state of being ruled by Aries. But that's not what happened. Your Scorpio rising spins your chart so that Scorpio is the sign of your first house. Gemini is seven signs away from Scorpio, making it the eighth house; so your sun is in the eighth house. Figure 9.2 shows what that looks like.

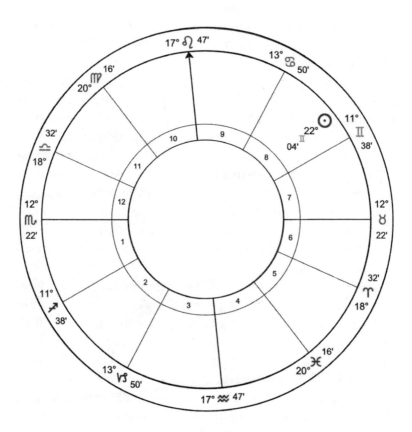

Figure 9.2. Sun and rising sign

Okay. Breathe. I know that might already seem like a lot. But let's just put together what we already know. We know that the eighth house represents death and rebirth, sex, things you own with your spouse or other people, other people's money, taxes, inheritance, psychic abilities, and taboo subjects. We know that Gemini is intellectual, chatty, witty, adaptable, curious (sometimes nosy), always thinking, and can be inconsistent or even superficial.

What you don't know yet is that the sun represents the true you. It's your essence—your inner self and the basis of your personality. Said another way, your inner self is Gemini. It's bright, communicative, curious, and all those delightful things Geminis are. Because your sun is in the eighth house, you'll experience those traits through the lens of the very heavy concerns of the eighth house. You're likely to be psychic, sexual, and very serious. Relationships will be a primary focus in your life and you'd prefer that they all be deep and intense. If they're not, you'll probably just move on. Your sun sitting in a house that is naturally Scorpio will make you have a very scorpionic personality. Because the issues of the eighth house are so intense, intense things will seem easier for you to handle than they are for most people. Things that might turn other people's worlds upside down could be no big deal to you. You're just used to that energy. But in the end, you're Gemini. So you'll still be smart, you'll still be chatty, you'll still be curious. But you might mostly be curious about the deep aspects of life.

The rising sign is often referred to as your mask. It's the metaphorical sunrise of your birth—the way you were lit up. It's how you present yourself to the world. It's also the cause of a lot of relationship breakups! (More on that in a second.)

In this chart example, you may very well be Gemini (sun sign), but you'll seem to all the world like a Scorpio (rising sign). It's the energetic mask that you wear in your everyday life. In this particular example, with an eighth house sun already making you seem scorpionic, even professional astronomers would likely guess you to be a Scorpio when they meet you. It can affect your basic attitudes about life as well as your appearance.

Oh, and those relationship problems? Well, think about this. You meet this great person, and you really, really like them! They're mysterious and sexy and kind of dark but in an enticing way. Oh my gosh, you think you're in love! (You've always loved Scorpios.) Then—oops. That person isn't Scorpio, they're Gemini with a Scorpio rising! The more you get to know them, the less mysterious and deep they become, and the more it bothers you that they just won't stop talking. You can't keep track of what they're talking about because they're constantly going from one subject to the next without warning. They just weren't who you thought they were, and the magic is gone.

By the way, they may be thinking the exact same thing about you if, for example, you're Leo with a Virgo rising. You weren't who you appeared to be either. But that's invisible to you. Just as the Scorpio mask they were wearing is invisible to them.

Some people have the same sun sign as their rising sign. I call this the "what you see is what you get" aspect. They aren't wearing an invisible mask. Keep in mind, however, that astrological charts are very complex. There can still be ways that a person isn't exactly who you think.

The third aspect of an astrological chart that people are likely to be aware of is what sign their moon is in. The moon represents your emotional self—in other words, it's how you experience the world through your feelings. How you respond to others at an emotional level, as well as your intuitive instincts about other people, are dictated by the sign and location of your moon in your chart.

BEYOND THE 12 SIGNS: THE PLANETS

Okay. The time has come to give you the last major part of all this: the planets. I didn't want to overwhelm you with that information, so we started with just houses and zodiac signs. Now it's time for the third dimension to all of this—these are all the signs you have (sun sign, moon sign, etc.), an explanation of each of the symbols you'll see in a full astrological chart.

Every person has all the worlds, the sun, and the moon in their chart, and each represents a different aspect of you. Each planet also has a glyph, or symbol, associated with it. This is to make it easier to fit upon an astrological chart. Some people (like me) have many planets huddled together on their charts. Printing the names of each planet would make for a very cluttered and difficult-to-read document. By using glyphs, this problem is diminished—though not always eliminated completely.

The following are all the planets and the nodes (north and south) along with what parts of your life, personality, and motivations they reflect about your life. For example, knowing where the sun is on your astrological chart (i.e., your sun sign) can reveal information about your true nature. The location of Venus will show how you interact in relationships. And so on.

The Sun: Your true nature; your essence, character, and ego; your inner self and personality

The Moon: Your emotions, feelings, and intuition; the unconscious and your instincts; how adaptable to change you are; your relationship with your mother and women in general

Mercury: Your intellect and how you communicate; the spoken and written word; how you learn and evaluate information; all rules of technology; business travel

Venus: Love, sociability, and the love of beauty; how you interact in relationships; romance, art, and physical beauty

Mars: Action where you're aggressive, passionate, and energetic; what drives you and makes you determined to act

Jupiter: Luck, optimism, hope, and faith; spirituality, expansion, and how you see life

Saturn: Restraint, challenge, being held back; where you're conservative and cautious; limitations, morality, and conscience; safety and security

Uranus: Rebellion, inspiration, new ideas; creativity; the place where epiphanies come from

Neptune: Imagination, dreams, mystical experiences; illusions, deception; drugs and addictions

Pluto: The unconscious; the way you handle power; upheaval and transformation; huge changes in life

North Node: What you're aspiring to accomplish in this lifetime; characteristics you're trying to learn and develop; the traits and work you're here to do; basically the opposite of the south node

South Node: What you've learned in past lives and perhaps overdone; you keep what you've learned, but you need to move away from the behavior of the sign of the south node and focus on the north node to grow and succeed

So let's look at just a teeny, tiny bit more detail on some sample charts.

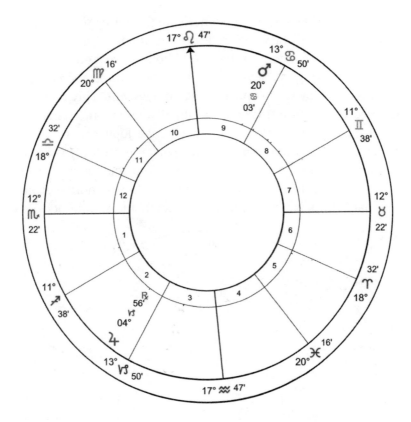

Figure 9.3. Mars and Jupiter chart

The chart in Figure 9.3 shows Mars in Cancer in the ninth house—what do we know? The ninth house is spirituality, travel, honesty, inspiration, being naturally happy, and all the things we outlined before. Cancer is loving, compassionate, intuitive, and focused on the family. Mars is where we take action. It's passionate, raring to go, and dedicated. Mars in Cancer is a challenging mix, because Mars wants to go, go, go on its own instincts, while Cancer is concerned about other people and is very dedicated to their desires. Cancer will mute the natural Mars fire. Mars in the ninth house, however, will mean that this person will be really dedicated to issues of spirituality, travel, and the rest. This will be where their passion is. And while Cancer mutes the aggressive tendencies of Mars, those tendencies might not be so terrible in the ninth house, where the focus is so spiritual.

Jupiter in Capricorn in the second house—what do we know? The second house is the sense of self-worth, self-esteem, material possessions, how you spend and treat money, and daily routines. Capricorn is great in this house, as it's all about finances, making money, and being cautious and conservative. Jupiter is expansiveness! Good luck and optimism. This person is probably going to do very well when it comes to prosperity and abundance.

Are you starting to see how this works? Here's another example that I think is important. It's the north and south nodes.

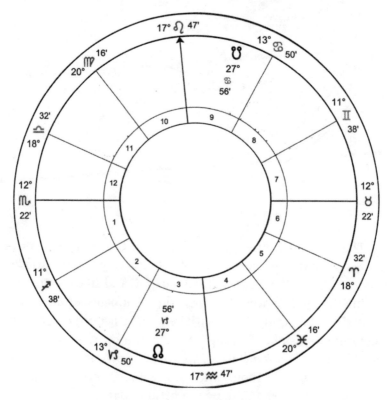

Figure 9.4. North and south nodes

The chart in Figure 9.4 shows the north node in Capricorn in the third house and the south node in Cancer in the ninth house. South node is what we've done lifetime after lifetime.

Enough already! Go be Capricorn (the opposing sign to Cancer). This person has overdone the taking care of others. They've been very focused on other people's needs and compassion and relying on their intuition. It's time to have some real-world experiences. Go be a banker, or maybe a stockbroker. Go create a big business and see what it feels like to accumulate some wealth. Learn something new! The soul is always wanting to learn something new. This chart has been designed to help this person be a success with that Jupiter in Capricorn in the second house.

All right. I've shielded you for as long as I can! Here's what a full-on chart looks like. But don't let it overwhelm you. Here goes . . . Take a look over at the chart in Figure 9.5.

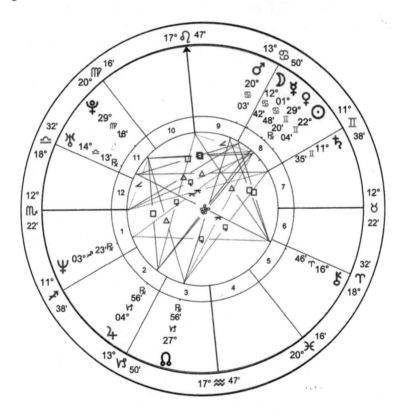

Figure 9.5. Full astrological chart

Are you okay? Are you still breathing? See, this is what I was telling you. Astrology is complex! Not only do you have all these planets all over the place, but their placement in the chart affects each other! That's too complicated to get into here, but when planets are close to one another (look at that eighth house!) or directly opposite from one another, they have an effect on each other. The location on the chart of a planet in relationship to another planet is called an aspect, and there are a bunch of different kinds.

All that I've shown you up to now is an example of a birth chart—the energies someone comes into life with. But there's also the power of where the planets are in the sky right now (or in the future) and how they relate to someone's birth chart. This is called a bi-wheel. It places where the stars are in the sky right now on top of the birth chart.

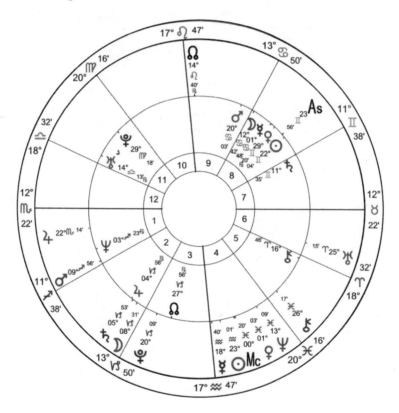

Figure 9.6. Bi-wheel chart

A professional astrologer would look at Figure 9.6 and see Saturn in the second house in the outer wheel floating over Jupiter in the inner wheel.

Figure 9.7. Saturn   Figure 9.8 Jupiter

The outer wheel is where the planets were at the time of this writing. The inner wheel is our imaginary birth chart. Saturn is sitting almost directly on top of that Jupiter in the birth chart. Conservative and restrictive Saturn would create a muting of the naturally jubilant and optimistic Jupiter during this time—possibly over finances. This person might also feel a little restless since Jupiter's expansiveness would be somewhat held back by Saturn. On the other hand, Saturn might help the person make some really sound choices that exuberant Jupiter might've overlooked. This is powerful information!

WHEN THINGS SEEM TO BE GOING BACKWARD

There's one last teeny thing I think I should mention before I move on. It's called a retrograde. You may have heard that term, especially as it pertains to the (in my humble opinion) much overdramatized Mercury retrograde.

Remember when we started this chapter, I told you that astrology isn't always about the actual movements of the planets, but how they *appear* to be moving. A retrograde is when a planet seems to be moving in reverse. Of course, the planets don't move backward in their orbits. But they can appear to do so based on their dance with Earth.

A retrograde tends to create—well—challenges. For example, you've already learned that Mercury rules communication, the written word (like contracts, for example), and technology. So when Mercury goes retrograde, there can be communication problems. You might sign a contract you wish you hadn't, and computers, cell phones, and other electronics might act up. These are things we work with regularly, and so people freak out when these things aren't working!

While it's understandable that all this makes Mercury retrogrades seem very intense, the key is to know how to work with them. Some people say to never sign a contract during Mercury retrograde. I would say instead to read it very, very carefully—and, as backup, maybe have a professional read it too. Be especially careful to communicate very thoroughly. Back up your files on your computer regularly.

Personally, I find the Mars retrograde to be way more challenging. What's Mars? It's action! Getting things done! I call the Mars retrograde the "running in the swimming pool" aspect, because that's what it feels like. It's three times as hard to get anything done. And so the best way to handle it is to plan for it. Know that during a Mars retrograde, things will go more slowly. Maybe plan a vacation during that time. And definitely try to avoid big deadlines during a Mars retrograde.

MANIFESTING WITH ASTROLOGY: WHEN YOU WISH UPON A STAR

There are several ways to use astrology to manifest things in your life. Knowing the energy of what's coming is powerful to be sure. But another way is called electional astrology (deciding the most appropriate time for an event).

When you create something new—say a business—you're choosing the astrological chart for that business. Say you're choosing the publication date of a book you just wrote. It'd be a good idea to choose a date and time that'd be particularly positive, right?

The same thing is true for a wedding. The time and day that you get married is the "birth" of the marriage and sets up the way the relationship will unfold.

For example, when Lee and I decided to get married, I sought out an astrologer to choose the date and time. This is how I found the astrologer I currently see. Not every astrologer does electional astrology, so it took me quite a while to find her.

When I found this astrologer, she asked me for a range of dates. What surprised me was that she didn't just ask me what city, she asked me for the actual street address! When we spoke next, she had more than one option, but one of the options was just particularly rosy—I mean *really* positive! It was so positive that Lee and I moved the time of our wedding from the afternoon to a brunch so that we could take advantage of that good fortune.

Neither of us had been married before, so we didn't know exactly what to expect. Friends were very sweetly telling us that little somethings will probably go wrong, but not to let it trouble us. It'd be wonderful all in all.

But nope. Not our wedding. It was flawless! It should've been cold, and we were worried snow would hamper things. But it was nearly 70 degrees, sunny, and gorgeous outside. It was one of the best days of our lives for sure! We wanted to do it all over again the next day. Astrology literally helped us manifest a perfect wedding.

NO. FREAKING. WAY.

I mentioned earlier that I like to get an annual reading each year around my birthday. So in December 2016, I contacted my favorite astrologer, and she prepared my chart for the next 12 months.

Of course, I already knew a lot about what was coming in 2017. My book *How to Be Your Own Genie* was launching. I also had a new tarot deck, *Animal Tarot Cards,* coming out that year. There was going to be a good bit of travel as well. None of this was information my astrologer knew of ahead of time, but still she spoke of travel and new creations at all the right times of the year. She was right on target. I call this validation. It not only shows that I'm on the course I think I'm on, but it also shows that the astrologer is spot-on. I can trust other things she says that I might not know of.

And sure enough, she started talking about something that was going to be happening in 2017. She had said that significant changes were coming, and I needed to be aware of and prepared for them. Now the thing was, even though I had all this validation from previous things she had said, the nature of the changes she saw coming sounded crazy to me. I thought, *No way! She's just a little off on this. This couldn't possibly happen.*

Well, guess what? It absolutely did happen. My astrologer also assured me that the effects would be temporary and that while it might sound scary, in the long run it'd be great for me.

So when big changes started to happen that seemed worrisome, I had the validation to rest upon to know, *This will all work out. It'll be okay.* I didn't worry. And I was prepared.

This is the power of astrology.

THE RAD-SCOOP ON ASTROLOGY

I love astrology. I think it's very important and can have a powerful effect in our lives. Knowing what energies are coming and how to work with them can be the difference between success and failure. It can be the difference between starting off on the right foot and falling flat on your face.

I've studied astrology since the late '90s. Even though I still consult professional astrologers, what I've learned benefits me in a couple of ways. When someone says Mercury retrograde is on the way, I know what to expect and I know what things to work on and what things to leave alone (if possible) until it's over. If someone tells me that Jupiter is affecting Venus in a positive way, I know it's time for a romantic getaway. Understanding the basics can really help you navigate the astrological freeways.

Having a basic knowledge of astrology also really helps when you do have a professional reading. You get more out of the reading because the astrologer isn't having to explain the nitty-gritty details.

However, if your desire is to learn astrology at a truly deep level, then my advice is to go all out. Study everything you can. Take classes. Find a mentor. There's a lot to learn, and it's multidimensional.

And you might just find this language of the Divine becomes a lifelong love affair.

CHAPTER 10

THE MAGIC OF NUMEROLOGY

IS NUMEROLOGY THE RIGHT CHOICE FOR YOU?

- Do you search for evidence of order in the Universe?
- Do you believe that there's an underlying structure to all things?
- Do you seek information about why you're here during this lifetime?

Numerology is a science founded upon the belief that numbers and sounds have a vibration in common that can give you important information about your true self as well as what the future holds. I once studied numerology rather extensively, but that was decades ago. So in doing research for this book, I really was seeing it with fresh eyes.

Every oracle I've explored in writing this compendium has had a distinctly different feel and focus. Numerology's energy felt like the science of astrology mixed with the subconscious connection of pendulums.

Before I go any further, there are a couple of things you need to know about numerology right up front.

First, there is math. I'm sure that can't possibly be a shock. However, it's very simple math. It's mostly just easy addition with occasional subtraction. There's no geometry or trigonometry for you to worry about. I admit that I used a calculator a couple times, but that's just because sometimes there were a lot of numbers to add up—not because it was difficult math.

Second, if you're familiar with the concept of angel numbers, which we touched upon in Chapter 2, please know that numerology is completely different. I do love angel numbers and use them all the time! But the meanings of angel numbers and numerology only occasionally agree with one another. Numerology has complex meanings for all the numbers, whereas angel numbers have very simplistic, and therefore easy to use, definitions. So if you think you already know about numerology because you understand angel numbers, keep reading, because there's a lot to learn and to gain from numerology.

The basis of numerology comes from calculations using your name and your birth date. The practice attributes numbers to the letters of the alphabet to transform your name into a number. Likewise, the numbers in your birth date get added together in various ways to provide information about yourself and the future.

Different numerologists disagree on what to call various calculations of numerology, but they generally agree on what information you're getting from the most common methods of transforming the various pieces of your name and birth date into numbers. For example, one of the primary calculations in numerology is to turn every letter in your full name into a number and then add them up. Some call this the expression number, but it can also be called the destiny number or simply the name number. However, the information it provides is largely the same for most numerologists. I happen to have a ridiculously long name, which is why I resorted to a calculator. But if your name is Susan Mary Jones, you should be fine with the simple math.

JUST A *LITTLE* HISTORY

Numerology (like astrology) is ancient and has turned up in most of the major civilizations. The Egyptians, Mayans, Hebrews, and even early Christians turned to numbers for answers about themselves and the Universe. Around 400 C.E., St. Augustine of Hippo is said to have written, "Numbers are the Universal language offered by the deity to humans as confirmation of the truth." Church leaders repeatedly banned numerology as an unaccepted practice, all the while using it in secret in conjunction with understanding religious texts. Evidence of Chinese numerology goes back 4,000 years.

Several versions of numerology still exist today, but the most common is the version called Pythagorean numerology (which is what I'll be sharing with you). It's loosely based upon concepts from his teachings that numerologists call the "science of numbers," which was presented to the world in the 6th century B.C.E. by (unsurprisingly) the Greek philosopher Pythagoras. His ideas formed a basis for the belief that numbers made up everything and had a powerful effect on the Universe. That makes it easy to see how he might then be credited as the "father of numerology," but in reality, he wasn't directly involved in the creation of contemporary numerology.

It's worth mentioning that the Chaldeans created a version of numerology that is older but also vastly more complicated and therefore less practiced today.

While many secret organizations like the Golden Dawn and the Masons were very interested in the meaning of numbers, the term *numerology* is a relatively recent word first used in 1907 by famed numerologist Dr. Julia Seton. The 20th century saw a big increase in interest in numerology among the general population, and there were several famous numerologists in the 1900s who shaped the science into the form it finds itself in today.

THE SECRET CODE OF YOUR LIFE PURPOSE

Numerology works on the principle that every number resonates to a particular frequency. It also states that everything
around us has a particular energy or vibration. Much like in
astrology, numerology relies on the concept that you chose the
date of your birth and that by working with those numbers, a lot
of information about who you are can be extracted.

Likewise, numerologists believe that you chose your name
before you were born on the basis of the vibration or energy
that you wanted to work with in this lifetime. That name was
relayed to the subconscious of your parents. Numerology works
using your full name: your first, last, and any middle name(s)
you may or may not have as reflected on your birth certificate.
By turning your full name into numbers, you can gain access to
information about your life purpose, your inner self, and other
important pieces of information.

Experts differ in opinion as to whether to take name changes
into consideration. Some numerologists are adamant that your
birth name is your birth name. Whatever is on your birth certificate is the final word, and name changes due to preference, marriage, or stage names are irrelevant. Other numerologists take
a softer approach, stating that a new name adds to the energy
of a birth name and can even be beneficial to how your life
flows. For example, taking a partner's name due to a marriage
can bring the energy of the ancestry of the partner into the life
of the person taking the new name.

For the sake of simplicity, I suggest working with your true
birth name. If numerology really speaks to you, check out the
suggested reading section at the end of the book for more expert
opinions as to how to handle name changes.

HOW IT ALL ADDS UP

Numerology can give you information on many aspects of
your life—including what your future holds at various times of

your life. However, in this compendium, we're going to be focusing on the most well-known numbers:

- The Life Path number
- The Expression number
- The Heart's Desire number
- The Personality number

Before we start doing math, let's talk about the meaning of the numbers themselves.

Numerology concerns itself with the numbers 1 through 9, 11, and 22. There are other numbers beyond these that some numerologists work with, but these are the primary ones. The numbers 11 and 22 are considered "master numbers" with special meanings of their own. The following is a short explanation of each number:

- **1:** The beginning, ambition, energetic, determined, focused, independent, go-getter, brave, originality, driven, the masculine

- **2:** Gentle, harmonious, supportive, considerate, sensitive, tactful, cooperative, loving, vulnerable, sincere, the feminine

- **3:** Artistic, creative, inspiring, imaginative, young at heart, confident, optimistic, enthusiastic, playful, joyful, insightful, fun

- **4:** Secure, scientific, rigid, structured, systematic, patient, practical, predictable, methodical, brilliant in business, trustworthy

- **5:** Visionary, spiritual, sensual, adventurous, explorer, constant change, dynamic, promoter, traveler, endlessly curious, insists on freedom

- **6:** Responsible, nurturing, teacher, selfless, loving, parental, dutiful, self-sacrificing, domestic, caring, sympathetic, healer, respectful

- **7:** Wise, scholar, analytical, charming, studious, scientific, meditative, focused, introvert, hermit, meditative

- **8:** Visionary, business oriented, prosperous, ambitious, controlling, political, successful, insightful, powerful, leader

- **9:** Humanitarian, philosopher, idealist, healer, self-sacrificing, kind, giving, writer, creative, artistic, completion

- **11:** The characteristics of 2 but intensified; extremely psychic, sensitive, and mesmerizing

- **22:** The characteristics of 4 but amplified; quite literally able to accomplish anything; exceedingly practical, with big plans

Now let's talk about names. Most numerologists are very strict about wanting to use your birth name—literally what's on your birth certificate. If you're adopted or for some reason don't know your actual birth name, numerologists will encourage you to seek it out through public records or adoption agencies. If your name has changed due to marriage or personal choice, they'll still use your birth name but also work with the new name as an "added energy" to your reading. A few numerologists will work with a changed name if it's been so incorporated into your psyche that you no longer even associate with or think of your birth name anymore.

All right. Math time. I'm going to use a very simple example: Susan Mary Jones, born March 28, 1990. I've chosen 1990 because 9s are very much like their description—self-sacrificing. You can add 9s into the calculation, or you can leave them out completely and still come up with the same eventual result. Also know that numbers are always reduced down to a single digit except for master numbers 11 and 22.

Life Path Number: Time for an example. Let's start by calculating the Life Path number. The Life Path number gives a broad understanding of how your life will play out. This includes the lessons you have come into this life to learn. For this reason, some numerologists call it the Life Lesson number.

The Life Path number is calculated using your birth date. The numerical values for each month through September are easy. January is 1, February is 2, and so on. The numerical value for October is 1 (1 + 0 = 1), November is 2 (1 + 1 = 2), and December is 3 (1 + 2 = 3).

Numerologists don't all calculate the Life Path number the same way, but I'll give you what I think is the most accurate. It requires you to reduce each piece of your birth date and then add them together. For Susan, it'd look like this:

Month: 3

Day: 2 + 8 =10; 1 + 0 = 1

Year: 1 + 9 + 9 + 0 = 19; 1 + 9 = 10; 1 + 0 = 1

Now you add the final three numbers together: 3 + 1 + 1 = 5. Susan's Life Path number is 5!

Remember how I told you that 9s always sacrifice themselves? Well, one useful trick to know is that we could've ignored those 9s in the equation and gotten the same result. If we eliminate the 9s in 1990, only adding together the 1 and the 0, and then reducing to 1, we still have the final calculation of 3 + 1 + 1 = 5.

Susan's Life Path number tells us that the life lessons she is here to experience are related to the qualities of the number 5. Susan is likely to be constantly seeking, always changing, always after the next big experience. Her experiences are likely to inspire others. She's likely to be a lot of fun, very interested in sensual experiences of all kinds, and quite spiritual! In fact, a search for spirituality is likely to be a big part of her explorations.

Some numerologists skip the part of reducing the month, day, and year and then adding the three numbers together. They'd just add all the numbers together (3 + 2 + 8 + 1 + 9 + 9 + 0) to get 32, and then add 3 + 2 to get the same answer of

5. The reason *not* to do it this way is that it can create a situation where you don't end up with a master number, whereas the original way I taught you could've ended in 11 or 22 for a different birthday.

The Life Path number isn't the only numerological calculation that involves your birth date. There are a lot of them. But let's turn our attention to Susan's name.

Pythagorean numerology turns your name into numbers. The numbers are as follows.

Figure 10.1. Pythagorean alphanumerology chart

Pretty easy right? The most commonly used calculations with a name involve turning the letters into numbers and adding them all up, then reducing down to one number, unless the letters of your name total up to one of the two master numbers, 11 or 22.

Expression Number: The Expression number (sometimes called your Destiny number) is the way you'll go about your life. It indicates the ways in which you react to situations or other people. It's your goals in life and the talents and characteristics —good and bad—that you were born with in order to handle those goals. It's created by turning all of the letters in your name into numbers and adding them up.

Heart's Desire Number: The Heart's Desire number is the true inner you. It's what drives you at your core. Sometimes called the Soul number, it's the authentic you that indicates your true motivations as you move through the world. It's calculated by adding up only the values of the *vowels* of your name.

Personality Number: Finally, the Personality number is sort of like your rising sign in astrology (see Chapter 9). It's the way you present yourself to the world. It's the public you that you don't mind showing to those around you. It's also how others see you. It's an important number, because you might find out you're not projecting yourself the way you think you are! It's calculated by adding up only the values of all the *consonants* in your name.

So let's take a look at Susan. I've created a chart, Figure 10.2, to make this as easy as possible.

Name	S	U	S	A	N	M	A	R	Y	J	O	N	E	S			
Expression (All Letters)	1	3	1	1	5	4	1	9	7	1	6	5	5	1	= 50	5 + 0 = 5
Hearth's Desire (Vowels)		3		1			1				6		5		= 16	1 + 6 = 7
Personality (Consonants)	1		1		5	4		9	7	1		5		1	= 30	3 + 0 = 3

Figure 10.2. Susan Mary Jones's chart

Susan's Expression number is 5—same as her Life Path number. Susan is constantly interested in learning. She enjoys travel and values her freedom deeply. She can get bored if there isn't something new to experience. Susan is aware of her own talents and she can really turn on the charm when she wants to.

Susan's Heart's Desire number is 7. On the inside, Susan is an introvert. She loves her time alone and is always thinking, always analyzing. She loves to learn, and in her free time she is probably either reading a book or researching something on the Internet. Not in the slightest bit shallow, Susan wants to understand the depths of any topic that interests her.

On the outside however, things are quite different for Susan. Her Personality number is a 3. Around people, she is likely to be an excellent communicator and quite charming. Fun to be around and endlessly optimistic, Susan will likely have many friends and be the life of the party (presuming she'd ever go to a party she didn't *have* to attend). She's likely to always look younger than her age, and in her natural desire to always see the positive in any situation, she might be a tad prone to exaggeration.

Susan is a very complex person. Her true nature is to be an introvert and experience the depth of life in her own little world. However, she knows that's not always possible, and so if she's going to be out in the world, she's going to turn on the charm so that people will give her what she wants. She's probably not being manipulative, but she is being very practical about how the world works.

MANIFESTING WITH NUMEROLOGY: TURNING MATH INTO MAGIC

Numerology is about cycles. Every year, month, week, and day of your life has a numerological value. These dates are called Personal Date numbers. Manifesting with numerology is about knowing those cycles and working *with* them, not against them. If you want to manifest more abundance in your life, that means understanding when the 8 cycles of your life are present and then taking the right action to match that. If you want romance or a family, you would work with the energy of the 2 and 6 cycles.

To calculate your Personal Year number, take your birthday month and day and add it to the last year in which you celebrated a birthday. Let's take our gal Susan as an example. Let's pretend it's November 2017. Therefore, Susan's last birthday was 3/28/2017. We simply take $3 + 2 + 8 + 2 + 0 + 1 + 7 = 23; 2 + 3 = 5$. This is a 5 year for Susan—she really likes 5s!

Susan would do well to focus on manifesting changes in her life that she's been wanting to make. Travel is also a good thing for Susan during this time. If there's any part of Susan's life that she's been wanting to break free from, a 5 year is the time.

A PINNACLE EXPERIENCE

Many years ago, when I was in my 20s, I was seeking a spiritual path. I was deeply into angels and tarot but also exploring astrology and numerology. What got me interested in numerology was a reading I received from an extremely talented numerologist.

Now, to give you an indication of how long ago this was, the reading was recorded on a cassette tape and given to me to keep. The reading was very accurate for where I was at that time in my life, but it also included something called Pinnacle Cycle numbers. These numbers pinpoint what your future life is going to be like in four stages, or pinnacles. I was still in my first pinnacle cycle at that time.

Many years later, while packing up to move into a new home, I stumbled upon that cassette tape. Naturally, I was curious, as I was well into my third pinnacle cycle by then. So I put it into a machine and hit PLAY.

Listening to that old cassette tape was a jaw-dropping experience. Everything that numerologist said about the last 20-something years of my life was completely spot-on! Including a cross-country move that I had no idea was coming at the time of the original reading, the end of a 14-year relationship that I thought was "forever," and a major career change!

THE RAD-SCOOP ON NUMEROLOGY

Numerology is a lot like astrology to me. It's the type of oracle where I like having the skill set in order to use pieces of it to plan for the energies that are coming. Things like Personal Year and Personal Month numbers can be very helpful. While it's easy enough to do the math, I also think a professional can be very helpful—especially in the beginning.

Even though it had been a long time since I'd worked with numerology, in all honesty, most of the numbers made perfect sense this time around. My Expression number is a 3, and it sounds exactly like me. My Life Path number is a 5, and that also feels spot-on. My Personality number also makes sense. In fact, next year's Personal Year number also made sense based on what I know I have coming up. However, my Heart's Desire left me confused. Everything I've read about it sounds like someone else.

As with astrology, I don't think you can take the Life Path, Expression, Heart's Desire, or Personality numbers as individual things. Like an astrological chart with planets flung in every direction, you have to take each of these numbers and their meanings and blend them. They have to be looked at as interacting with one another. They relate to one another.

When I took that into consideration, that Heart's Desire number became a lot clearer to me.

CHAPTER 11

THE MAGIC OF MEDITATION

IS MEDITATION THE RIGHT CHOICE FOR YOU?

- Are you stressed out?
- Would you like to have more peace in your life?
- Would you like to improve your health?
- Would you like to increase your ability to hear messages from the Divine?

Reasons (aka excuses) not to meditate:

- I don't have time.
- I can't sit still.
- My mind won't shut up.
- I'm fine. I don't need it.
- My mind won't shut up.
- I can't make it work.
- MY MIND WON'T SHUT UP!

Confessions of a spiritual teacher: Before I did the research for this book, I didn't meditate. No seriously, I didn't. Like . . . at all. Those reasons up there? Those were *my* reasons (excuses). It wasn't that I'd never tried. I'd tried many times. But here's how it would go for me:

Me: Okay. Just going to meditate for 20 minutes. Focusing on breath.

Mind: *This is dumb. You can't do this. Shouldn't you be writing?*

Me: Back to breath. Bringing focus back to breath.

Mind: *Lunch was good yesterday. Britney has a new album! Palm Springs . . .*

Me: Geez. Okay. Back to breath. Breathing. Quieting mind . . .

Mind: *Quieting mind? Who do you think you are, Deepak Chopra?*

Me: Back to breath. Back to breath. Focus on the breath.

Mind: *Hey! Ya know what? Christmas is coming!*

Me: OMG! Christmas *is* coming! Oh cool! Wait! No!!! Back to breath.

Mind: *Hey, Mickey, you're so fine! You're so fine you blow my mind!*

Me: Hey, Mickey! Agh—stop! Oh surely it's been 20 minutes . . .

Mind: *(Snickering) It's only been five.*

Does that perhaps sound like your experience? All it took was two or three attempts with that kind of mind chatter for me to decide that meditation just wasn't something I could do. Chances are also pretty good that you've never had *any* experience with meditation. At the time of this writing, only 8 percent of people in the United States practice meditation.

The benefits to using meditation are, frankly, astonishing. Here are just a few:

- You become more creative.

- It lowers your blood pressure.

- It increases feelings of happiness.

- It reduces stress and worry.

- It improves memory and the ability to think clearly.

- You develop a healthier immune system.

- It helps you understand what's really important in life.

- You're able to handle stressful situations more easily.

And that's just a tiny part of the list.

But why include meditation in a book on talking to the Divine? Because meditation increases your intuition! It allows messages from the Universe that can help you live a happier life to make their way into your noggin. And that, after all, *is* what this book is about.

What I discovered in my research for this chapter is that most of us who try meditation take something immensely simple and make it extremely hard. The trouble we create for ourselves is by thinking it has to be a certain way, and if we don't get it right, then we're just not built for this, and we quit. Self-judgment and a lack of understanding of the process is where we fail.

Actually, that's true for life in general.

To succeed at meditation, you have to stop judging yourself and just keep trying.

Remember that me-versus-my-mind conversation I started this chapter with? The truth is, I was actually doing exactly what I should've been doing. When thoughts came through, I would notice them, let them drift by, and then return to focusing on my breath. Where I messed up was in judging the "success" of my efforts.

With meditation, you just never know what's going to float through your head. Happy memories, worries and fears . . . honestly, the goofiest of things can float in and then out. The trick is to acknowledge those thoughts and then return your focus to your breath. The *real* trick is to not judge those thoughts. Thoughts should be allowed to drift by like clouds on a summer day.

You don't judge the clouds, do you?

JUST A *LITTLE* HISTORY

As with most traditions that go back thousands of years, there's debate about just how old meditation is. The first written records talking about meditation come from India around 1500 B.C.E. However, archaeologists have come across paintings on walls showing people in what appears to be the very traditional position for meditating. Those images go back somewhere between 5000 and 3000 B.C.E. I know that's a pretty wide time frame, but archaeologists and historians don't agree on the date.

What historians do agree on is that meditation really started to be more widely documented between the 6th and 5th centuries B.C.E. The Buddhists in India considered meditation to be a very important part of their belief system. Taoists of China were also practicing meditation.

The history of meditation shouldn't be looked at as just an Eastern religious practice. In the Middle Ages, Judaism practiced forms of meditation as a part of prayer. Variations related to Kabbalah were also practiced. Christian mysticism also had types of prayer that could be considered a form of meditation upon the words of God.

For Western culture, meditation started to become more widely known in the 18th century. By the early 1900s, two books were published that brought meditation even more into people's awareness: an English translation of the Tibetan *Book of the Dead* and Hermann Hesse's *Siddhartha*.

In the United States and Europe, meditation gained more attention in the 1960s, when transcendental meditation became popular. Though *popular* is a very relative term, since still only a very small percentage of people in Western society meditated.

Meditation actually has modern science and medicine to thank for the current attention it has in Western culture. The many health benefits and the growing awareness that meditation isn't necessarily a religious practice have increased the number of people meditating. The fact that it's also been shown to help people with chronic pain and reduce stress has caught people's attention as well.

BUCKLE UP! WE'RE GOING FOR A RIDE!

I love cars. I also love metaphors. (Guess where we're headed?)

Scientists say that there are five categories of brain waves: gamma, beta, alpha, theta, and delta.

Let's talk about the first one: gamma. It's the equivalent of you driving your car 100 miles per hour. Your radio is set to heavy metal music. You're on the interstate and there's a bunch of other people in cars also going 100 miles per hour, so you're alert! Actually, you're not just alert, you're noticing every little thing, and if it gets to be too much, you start to freak out. This is the category of brain waves when you're really ramped up, actively focused on trying to learn things, or very much engaged in a topic.

In the next category of brain waves, beta, you just took the exit off the interstate. You slow the car to a standard 55 miles per hour on a local highway. You change the radio to a pop rock station. You're not freaking out anymore. You're just taking a drive. This is the category of brain waves you're usually in when you're just going through a regular day.

The next category, alpha, is when you pull the car off the highway to drive a leisurely 25 miles per hour through a lovely park. You change the radio station to one playing a Barry Manilow marathon and then quickly change the station again to one playing soft jazz. This is the category of brain waves where you feel at peace. Relaxed. Everything is fine.

You find a nice place to park the car under a tree, and you change the radio station to New Age meditation music. Guess why? Right! This is the category of brain waves, theta, where meditation can happen. You close your eyes and just relax. You concentrate on breathing and the meditation music and whatever thoughts just float by.

The last category of brain waves, delta, means you just fell asleep at the wheel. But who cares? You're safely parked, and the radio station changes itself to 101.1 WGOD. This is the state of brain waves where we sleep or dream. But lifelong meditators can reach this state and still be awake. (Wow!)

So meditation basically takes your brain, gets it off the interstate, and slowly brings you to that lovely place where your car is parked under a tree while you listen to music that lets you drift into a place where you're more psychic, more at peace, and, well . . . happy!

PILLOWS FOR PEACE

So you think you'd like to try meditation . . . That's great! I promise, if you give it a real chance, you'll *love* the results. There is a little bit of prep work. Not much, but like anything new you try, it works best if you make a commitment to it.

Experts on meditation say that your chances of creating a successful meditation practice increase if you do it every day at the same time and in the same place. That's not to say you'll fail if you can't do that. You won't. But it's easier if your body and mind know that there's a regular schedule.

Many people find first thing in the morning to be the right time. You're less likely to nod off during meditation first thing in the morning, and it really sets you up to have a great day! Others find it's best to do when they come home from work so that they can release whatever happened during the day. You choose the best time for you, the time that is likely to let you succeed.

You don't need special clothes, but you do need to be comfortable. Some people sit on a pillow on the floor cross-legged, but you don't have to. You can sit in a chair if you prefer. But it's best if the back of the chair is straight.

You'll need a special place where you won't be disturbed. Some people like incense or meditative music. Electronic devices should be turned off or silenced so as not to disturb you during your meditation practice. If you're using a smart device for meditation music, make sure all notifications are turned off.

When you're first starting out, you might want to try meditating for 10 to 20 minutes every other day. If you can only handle 5 minutes, that's fine, but try for 10 to 20. Once you start to get the hang of it, you'll love the results so much, you'll be meditating every day pretty quickly.

Once you've established the when and the where, it's time to give it a go. But first, repeat after me:

"I won't judge myself or this experience.

"Thoughts coming and going is normal. When they occur, I'll just return my attention to my breathing.

"This is worth my time.

"I'm excited about this opportunity for more inner peace and a better connection with the Divine.

"I won't judge myself or this experience."

What you're doing here is what I finally gave in and did for myself—giving yourself the chance to succeed at meditation.

Get comfortable and close your eyes. Pay close attention to your breath. If you realize the position you thought was going to be comfortable isn't so comfortable after all, then no problem.

Just shift or change it altogether until it is. Meditation is an act of self-kindness. That's important to remember.

Take a few deep breaths, and then let your breath go to its natural state. If you're nervous or have had some anxiety already in your day, you might find yourself breathing very shallowly or even holding your breath. By keeping your attention on your breath, you can release that anxiety so that you can breathe normally.

As you sit there, thoughts are going to come through. Some thoughts will be of the past, others of the future. It might be difficult at first to let go of what's just been happening or something that is on your schedule later that day. Just try to go back to focusing on your breath.

What did I say? "Meditation is an act of self-kindness." If things from the past that you regret come up, forgive yourself and go back to your breath.

Judging your initial success or beating yourself up for how things are going isn't helpful. It's also pointless. Be kind. Go back to your breath.

When the time you have set aside for meditation is up, just bring your focus back to the here and now and open your eyes.

If you feel more peaceful and grounded than you did when you started, then hooray! Try to take that feeling with you into whatever you do after meditation.

If you're still just getting used to it, congratulate yourself for sitting for the allotted time and resolve to try again tomorrow or the next day.

In time, you'll find the ability to quiet your mind and allow messages from Source to drift into your awareness. If you have a particular issue you want assistance with, hold the intention as you begin your meditation that the Universe will provide clarity or even the answer you've been looking for!

But please do yourself a favor: Keep going. Keep trying. If something distracts you, start over without an unkind word for yourself. You *will* get there if you just keep going.

MANIFESTING WITH MEDITATION: THE GIFT OF PRESENCE

The three primary ways through which meditation helps you manifest your desires are the Law of Attraction, clarity that comes from your subconscious, and Divine inspiration.

When you meditate upon what you're wanting to create, you allow for bits of brilliance buried in your subconscious to drift into your consciousness. These epiphanies can be locked away when you're stressed, concerned about the anxieties of "reality," and unfocused due to too many obligations. Meditation allows all of that to be cleared away so new ideas or solutions to problems can come into your awareness.

As I've said before, meditation also increases your intuition and allows the Universe not only to provide you with Divine insight but also to work with you via the Law of Attraction to manifest your desires. Meditation provides clarity of desire, optimism for the future, a powerful sense of worthiness, and the ability to assess situations to make the right choices. All of these work with the Law of Attraction to bring what you want into your reality.

DESIGNING A MORE PEACEFUL LIFE

Ted is a senior electrical designer living in Knoxville, Tennessee. Three years ago, his life wasn't really going the way he wanted it to. His high-stress job made him a "grumpy bear" on Sundays as he dreaded going back to work. A crisis at work (of which there were many) could almost cause him to fall apart.

At the same time, Ted had been searching for a spiritual path. He identified as Christian, but church and the religion itself provided little in terms of comfort or support. He also felt that the church simply didn't have the answers to his questions. He knew there had to be something more.

He craved peace and a true connection with the Divine.

At that time, he met a new friend who was deeply spiritual, and she introduced him to *A Course in Miracles*. He started a regular study of the course and began to read books by Neale Donald Walsch and Don Miguel Ruiz. Ted and his new friend started talking more and more, having lunch together nearly every day. Suddenly, Ted realized he was on the spiritual path that he'd so desperately desired. His friend recommended meditation and explained the steps to Ted. After three or four months of talking about it, Ted decided to give it a try.

Immediately, Ted's life started to change. His anxiety faded away and his thought processes became clearer and more guided. He stopped getting angry about things so easily and it made a huge difference in how he handled crises at work. Ted's wife and children also noticed a big difference in his behavior and how he interacted with them.

Once Ted realized the tremendous benefits of meditation, he didn't want to stop. Ted's wife transformed a spare bedroom into a meditation space for him. It became a daily practice. His friend recommended some video and audio guided meditations for him, and he enjoyed them.

Still, Ted wasn't quite sure if he was "doing it right." And so, in December 2016, Ted took a seminar on meditation, only to realize that he was indeed doing it perfectly. Soon, Ted began to receive messages about things in his life that were about to happen that were completely accurate! His marriage also became stronger, and he and his wife grew closer.

Today, Ted is happier than he's ever been. He has the close connection to Source that he'd always craved, and he feels at peace almost all of the time. This is the magic of meditation!

THE RAD-SCOOP ON MEDITATION

Meditation is amazing! It almost defies explaining, because if you aren't meditating, then you're probably operating at a state of constant input and low-level anxiety that you aren't even aware of. It's only once you start to meditate that you become aware of just how wound up you are all day, every day.

It also definitely increases your connection with the Divine, angels, fairies, your inner self—whatever you're looking for. It can hook you up!

Listen. Just between you and me. Just little ol' Radleigh and you. Trust me. Try it. If you've tried it in the past, and it didn't work out, try it again. Just give it a go.

Okay? Pinky promise? Cool.

CHAPTER 12

THE MAGIC OF MANTRAS

ARE MANTRAS THE RIGHT CHOICE FOR YOU?

- Are you seeking a straight-up direct connection to Source and your true inner self?

- Would centuries-old and proven ways to manifest your wishes be of interest?

- Is seeking a connection to Source something you're willing to put a lot of time into?

- Please keep reading even if you don't. Because this is powerful stuff and you owe it yourself to at least know it exists.

Words are powerful. If I were going to sum up mantras in three words, that's how I'd do it. I believe many people think mantras and meditation are close to the same thing or that meditation is a required part of mantras, but they really are separate concepts.

If you're unfamiliar with what mantras are, they're usually a few words or a phrase (though a mantra can be just a single word) most often spoken in the ancient language of Sanskrit.

They're tied to Hinduism, though they also exist in Buddhism and other belief systems.

What mantras *aren't* are affirmations. When I reached out to my friends in the spiritual community for their stories about mantras, I was really surprised at how many of them thought that affirmations and mantras were the same thing. Every single person who told me they worked with mantras followed up with something like "I use them every day! My current mantra is 'I am infinitely loved.'"

Um . . . no. That's not a mantra. But it *is* an affirmation.

Affirmations are positive phrases, set in the first person and in the present tense, that people repeat to themselves when they're wanting to manifest something in particular or comfort themselves. An affirmation might be "I am abundant in all things" or "There's a reason for everything that happens." They aren't tied to any particular deity, are spoken in your native language, and generally do not require a daily practice. Affirmations are magical in their own right, and I definitely want to talk to you about them! However, mantras are an entirely different practice from affirmations. Ironically, in order to find people truly practicing mantra, I had to reach out to my students!

Mantras are believed to have spiritual, almost magical, powers. They're also seen as a way to work with the psyche to change your perceptions of the world and your life (and therefore your reality).

Taking the explanation to the next level, mantras are particular phrases set to tones or musical notes called a raga. They can be chanted either aloud or in your mind. They aren't prayers per se, but a way to tune in to spiritual energy. A particular mantra might invoke a deity, create a more powerful spiritual life, ward off danger, or just help with concentration. Used in their purest form, they're meant to bring you closer to the Divine—to God—so that you can realize your highest self, balance karmic issues, and end the cycle of reincarnation so that you can return to Source. Those wishing to make this their life's work can spend eight hours a day moving between mantras, meditation, and prayer, for years. Some chant mantras for *decades*.

Mantras are tied to deities such as Krishna, Shiva, Kuan Yin, or Buddha. Some consider the *Ave Maria* to be a kind of mantra for Mother Mary, although that is probably more like a prayer.

It isn't a requirement to follow Hindu or Buddhist philosophy to work with mantras. Though if your purpose in using mantras is enlightenment and to see God, it's likely that you would shift into those belief systems. If your purpose is less lofty and more along the lines of finding a more peaceful life or manifesting a life partner, then you can use mantras with whatever belief system you already have.

You've probably heard the term *guru*. A guru is meant to refer to someone who's attained a high level of success with mantras. A guru should be someone who has successfully invoked the full power of a mantra, leading them closer to God. They now have that power within them to access as they see fit. I say "should be" because fake gurus are sadly common and true gurus incredibly difficult to find in this day and age.

If you were to seek a guru and find a true one, the two of you would most likely spend a year or more together making sure you're right for one another. A guru might decide what the right mantra for your training is during that time.

The guru-disciple relationship is extremely powerful and not something to be entered into lightly. A guru may decide to "initiate" you, literally placing some of the power of their mantra within you. In the Hindu belief system, you and the guru are now linked not only in this life but in all lives. You're also linked to your guru's guru, and the guru before that. It's easy to see how that makes this relationship an extremely weighty choice.

While it's believed to be preferable to find a guru to help you work with with mantras, it's absolutely not required that you do. As I said, true gurus are quite rare these days, and there are a lot of fake gurus running around creating problems for unsuspecting students or would-be disciples.

The other thing that is crucial to know is that teachers and experts in mantras insist that if you don't believe in God, and especially the Hindu or Buddhist Gods, then you're wasting your time with mantras. By their very nature, they're tools of faith meant to lead you through the power of a deity to the ultimate All That Is. If you don't believe, then it's a bit like buying a toaster but not having electricity in your home—there's nothing to power it. Each mantra is linked to a specific deity, so if you don't believe in that deity, then you're also not going to get very far.

JUST A *LITTLE* HISTORY

When you look at the history of mantras and meditation, a lot of the time line sounds alike. That's because the reference material for them travels through the same belief systems. They're believed to be at least 3,000 years old, although Vedic priests insist they're far older than that. Still, the earliest mantras are said to come from the Rig Veda dating back to 1500 B.C.E.

Initially, mantras were taught only within the Vedic priests' circles and were handed down orally. Eventually, they began to be written down, which is how they went from the spoken word to Sanskrit.

Mantras are said to have been discovered (as opposed to created) by great seers thousands of years ago. These seers are called rishis. The sounds of the mantras and the spiritual energy they have were discovered through the rishis' spiritual practices, and then shared with others. It could be said that mantras are the music of the Universe. Those who chant mantras sing along until that music becomes a part of who they are.

THE POWER OF SOUND

The word *mantra* at its simplest level means "sound." Sound is vibration. When someone is chanting a mantra, it's not just about the chanting, it's about trying to become the sound. It's about activating different parts of the body and the mind to align with what ancient Vedic priests determined would connect you with the spiritual energy that'd provide the desired effect. Mantras are literally considered a science in the Hindu belief system.

Countless people have used these same mantras for thousands of years to connect with the Divine, manifest what they want in their lives, or protect them from danger. Think of the power that kind of focused energy would create! Those who dedicate their life to this spiritual practice open themselves up to that Divine energy, and it becomes a part of them. It can take years of unending, dedicated practice, but once they've been successful, they become a part of the mantra, and the mantra becomes a part of them.

AND ON THE SEVENTH DAY . . .

Throughout this compendium, I have provided you with real stories from real people (including me) about experiences with various oracles and belief systems. As I wrote the chapter on mantras, I felt a little concerned. Of all the topics, mantras certainly demand the most from you. They also could arguably have the greatest reward. Nevertheless, I worried that I was making the practice of mantra seem unworkable for daily life. Because of that, I decided to share *two* real stories within this chapter so that you can read for yourself just how powerful and uplifting working with mantras can be. Here now is a story from Priti Mistry (you first met her in Chapter 7 on pendulums) about how mantras have helped her life. (The second story will come later in the chapter.)

I'm sharing my early experience with mantras. Over a decade ago, I started taking meditation seriously. I started practicing one of the techniques that I'd learned from my teacher. It's called *Manas Havan*, or *Havan* meditation. *Havan* is where you create a holy fire, chant a mantra, and go on offering oil, ghee, or other *Havan* ingredients to the fire. *Havan* is done with a specific intention to manifest or achieve something, whether material or spiritual. In *Manas Havan*, we visualize the process instead of actually doing it.

The ritual asked me to chant a mantra 108 times in meditation. The mantra I chose was *Om Narayan Narayan Arpan Namaha. Swaha!* We say *Swaha* after each chant, as we make an offering to the fire. The meaning of this mantra roughly is "Dear God (Narayana), I surrender and merge my Divinity in you. We're both one now." My only intention and deep desire was to connect to my higher self.

The first three days saw me getting worked up and stressed while meditating because I was totally focused on counting. (Remember, 108 times.) It became like an academic ritual, and I hate rituals.

On the fourth day, I told myself, *No more counting! I want to enjoy the process and not get stressed. That's it!* That's when I stepped into magic—or, rather, allowed magic to touch me. I enjoyed being in that space for as long as my heart desired.

On the seventh day, I could sense and see a ball of light hovering above my head. I wondered what it could be. Well, lo and behold, I received an answer through my thoughts! *I am your higher self!* It was a deep and reassuring voice. I was dumbstruck and ecstatic and experienced myriad emotions. I hadn't expected to connect so soon . . . not in my wildest dreams!

What followed next was simply magical. I started receiving healing energy and guidance from my higher self without even asking for it. I became an observer and simply acted on the guidance. At that time, I had no idea that I was supposed to help others connect with their own higher self, for healing, protection, and guidance. It's been a wonderful journey of living from my heart.

There's one more mantra that I chant often—while walking, cooking, or doing just about anything. That is the Gayatri mantra. It helps me get focused and grounded instantly:

Om Bhur Bhuva Swaha

Tatsavitur Vareniyam

Bhargo devasya dhimahi

Dhiyo Yo naha Prachodayat.

CHANT, CHANT, CHANT, REPEAT

As I mentioned earlier, mantras are generally chanted repeatedly until the desired outcome has occurred. There are books that share mantras for particular purposes, such as abundance, removing blocks, or romance. Mantras take time, dedication, and passion. Any particular change you wish to make with mantras is likely to require a minimum of six weeks to accomplish. During that time, you would need to set aside perhaps one or two hours at least twice a day for chanting. A mantra might require being chanted 108 times (like Priti's) or 1,000 times! You might be asked to chant for 40 days, or a mantra might require 960 days!

This chanting can't be mindless. It requires that you're focused, emotionally and mentally involved, and devout. Even if you're doing extra chanting while washing the dishes, your mental focus still has to be on the mantra. This is where meditation and mantra are alike. They require a commitment that can be challenging to remain loyal to until you've really made it a habit.

Most people will have a special space or altar where they practice their mantras. It's said to be best to do it during the time just before the sun rises and right after it has set. It's customary to take a bath or shower and to put on fresh clothing before beginning the chant.

Choosing a mantra is important. If you have a real guru, they may give you a mantra based on what you wish to accomplish. But that's rare these days, so you'll probably need to choose one for yourself. As I said, there are books that describe mantras based on your desires. Mantras cover a vast array of topics, from spiritual insights to self-confidence, physical and mental healing, and ridding yourself of unwanted emotions.

If the practice of mantra is for you, it'll lift you up, make you happy, sometimes bring up unexpected emotions that you can heal, and generally be a pleasant experience. You might learn a mantra and be so pleased that you just don't want to stop saying it.

Or you might find mantras to be just more than you wish to commit to right now.

HAPPY BIRTHDAY

Jagdeep Mangat was going through a difficult phase and was truly trying to understand the meaning of life, manifest abundance, evaluate her relationships, and discover what was generally for her highest good. Here, in her own words, is her magical story about mantras:

> One day while meditating, I felt a presence. It felt very real to me, as if someone were right next to me, blessing me. My whole body went very hot, and I felt dizzy with the high energy that was present. Through my third eye, I was shown that it was none other than Ganesh, the Hindu God of good fortune. I bowed my head out of respect and love, and tears began to flow down my cheeks. My soul had yearned for such a blessing.
>
> The same day, I had a strong inclination toward listening to mantras. As I often do, I pressed the SHUFFLE button on my mantra playlist and said aloud, "Please play the mantra that is for my highest good." The random mantra that played was *Om Gam Ganapataye Namaha*, the mantra to remove obstacles that is sung for Lord Ganesh. I closed my eyes and immersed myself in the mantra. I felt my soul, body, and mind immersed in the love that was showered on me by Lord Ganesh, and I in turn was filled with gratitude.

Ganesh is the god who helps to remove all obstacles in life and is called upon to bless new projects or when anything new in life is started, such as a business. I didn't pay much attention to why I was being drawn toward this particular God. I said my gratitude and thanks to him for being there for me.

The next day, I was meditating outside under a tree. Immediately after meditation, I saw a white rat on the fence. Now, in my 18 years of being in this house, I have never seen a rat near my house. And yet, the rat is Ganesh's vehicle in Hindu beliefs. I just looked at it and thanked Ganesh for sending it to me as a blessing from him. I recognized it as another way that Ganesh was sending me the message that he was here with me.

The same thing happened the next day and the day after that. I said my gratitude and started to ponder why I was being shown Ganesh every day.

This continued for a week. I finally put two and two together when I realized that Ganesh Chaturthi, Ganesh's birthday, was coming up. Right up to Ganesh Chaturthi, every day I would either stumble upon a photo of Ganesh or would switch on the radio and hear Ganesh mantras or receive messages on Facebook or my phone about him.

I opened my heart and welcomed him into my life. Why wouldn't I? A deity was connecting with me to show me the way to life. Instead of now pondering and wondering about it, I just let go of all control and welcomed him into my life. I felt so relieved that a God that clears obstacles was there with me, saying to me, "I'm here, and I'll help you."

On the day of Ganesh Chaturthi, not only was I blessed with financial abundance but also many internal mental blocks and old belief systems and fears were eradicated. My relationships started to bloom. I felt truly blessed.

Since that day, I've bought a little idol of Ganesh and pray to him every day to remove any obstacles in my life and to assist in my soul growth. I also continue to sing *Om Gam Ganapataye Namaha* for him. Simply saying "I give all my worries to you Ganesh, and I know you'll take care of them" helps me in my life.

I'm truly grateful, Lord Ganesh, for you being a part of my journey and my life, holding my hand and guiding me. Thank you.

MANIFESTING WITH MANTRAS: CHANTING WITH THE OLDIES

Manifesting with mantras is basically the same practice as the spiritual path of mantras. You may or may not spend hours a day in practice; hopefully, it won't take you the years that the enlightenment of self-realization takes in the spiritual practice. The rest, however, is the same. It's a daily recitation in a focused and prayerful way of the appropriate mantra for what you're wanting to create.

To give you an idea, here is an example of what a true mantra would look like for the purpose of bringing good luck into your life:

Om Sharavana Bhavaya Namaha

(pronounced "Om Shah-rah-vah-nah Bhah-vah-yah Nah-mah-ha")

Here is an example of a mantra for abundance and prosperity:

Om Shrim Maha Lakshmiyei Swaha

(pronounced "Om shreem mah-ha lahk-shmee-yay swah-ha")

And here's a mantra for meditation and spiritual self-realization:

Om Namah Shivaya

(pronounced "Om Nah-mah Shee-vah-yah")

AFFIRMATIONS

Affirmations are sort of Mantra-Lite. Louise Hay's pioneering work in affirmations brought them to the attention of most of the New Age world during the course of her life. Can you use affirmations to manifest things? I believe you can. I think they're directly tied to the Law of Attraction, and they can definitely help you rewire your noggin from a place of negative chatter to a place of . . . well . . . positive chatter!

And positive chatter means happy outcomes.

THE MONEY MAGNET

My friend Joanie Light is a big-time affirmation practitioner. Affirmations have always been a part of her manifestation techniques, from creating peace in her life to manifesting material goods. Here's what Joanie had to share about affirmations:

> The first affirmation I ever learned was the oldie but goodie from Émile Coué, dating back to the 1800s. "Every day in every way, I am getting better and better" has always been a simple affirmation to manifest anything in my life that I wanted to be better, including finances, health, and happiness.
>
> I have used affirmations to deepen meditation and get in touch with a deeper spirituality. Repeating "I am love" or "I am peace" while meditating can enhance a spiritual connection to the Divine.
>
> When my husband and I started our business, the early months were tough. Our cash flow wasn't flowing yet. Rather than panicking about our bills not getting paid, I would meditate and repeat the affirmation "We are magnets to money. Money flows easily to us." During my meditation, I would visualize a shower of $100 bills raining down on us. Sometimes as quickly as the next mail delivery, we would receive multiple payments from clients or letters containing discounts on bills that gave

us a zero balance. The key was not putting limits on how money would appear and giving thanks for what we had received.

It's just as easy to affirm abundant health, loving relationships, or joyful lives. Even when something pops up in my life that is worrisome or difficult to face, I affirm, "Out of this situation, only good can come."

THE RAD-SCOOP ON MANTRAS

So. This is what I think about mantras. I think the practice is powerful, amazing, and ancient spiritual work that can absolutely bring you right up, nice and personal, to the Divine. If that is what you're looking for . . . if what you want is to really see God and know a kind of bliss and self-realization most of us never experience, then you should be signing up for mantra class. I'm rather tempted to call mantras the ultimate language of the Divine because of that very possibility.

I also believe mantras *can* help you manifest your wish list. But they come with the price of big-time commitment. I think that if you're using mantras for your spiritual "go touch the Divine" quest, then as you proceed on that journey, you can probably use the manifesting mantras rather quickly.

However, if you aren't on that quest . . . if you don't have a lot of time to invest in mantra work . . . then maybe affirmations or one of the other methods in the compendium would be better for you.

ENDINGS AND BEGINNINGS

We think of the world as being a very big place and our civilization as being incredibly old. Of course, neither of those is true—at least not from the view of the Universe. Earth is actually kind of itty-bitty compared to other worlds out there, and humankind's impact has been just a blink-of-an-eye sort of thing.

And yet . . . just look at the amazing and magical things we have created. Some of the most wondrous gifts that came from the human race were created by tapping into the Divine magic within all of us and reaching out to Source to say, "Hey there! We're here! We love you. *Please* talk to us."

And God does talk to us. If we take the time to listen, practice our Divine skills, and give that conversation the devotion it deserves, we immediately find out that the Universe is extremely chatty. We may be reaching out, but Source is also reaching right back to us.

In this compendium, I have tried to show you several ways to make that connection a lot easier. Yet I have not even begun to scratch the surface on the infinite ways we humans have devised to connect with the Divine and manifest the joy and happiness we deserve.

For me, this journey has been both enchanting and challenging, rewarding and enlightening, fun and also humbling. My eyes have been opened in ways I never dreamed of. Honestly, I don't know why I've been so surprised. I've known that life is magic for quite a long time now. What was I expecting?

As we come to the end of our journey through *Compendium of Magical Things*, may you find new beginnings that open your eyes to the magic within you and out in the world. Go talk to angels or fairies! Learn the language of tarot or Lenormand! Put a pendulum in your pocket for instant answers! Discover the ancient secrets that are yours for the asking from the runes or the I Ching! Unlock the personal insights available from astrology or numerology! Find the peace and spiritual enlightenment just waiting for you via meditation and the practice of mantra! Or let this journey guide you to other oracles not covered in this compendium. The possibilities are endless.

Of course, I am hopeful that you will try as many of these oracles as you feel called to. I have experienced an almost child-like delight as each one of them validated the other and gave me information to ponder. But if reading this book has done nothing else, I hope that it has shown you that there is no "one way" to God. There is no singular path that leads to Goddess that is the "right" way. Everyone's spirituality is perfectly their own. As I said in Chapter 1, we're all returning to the All That Is because there is nowhere else to go.

Tread lightly if habits from childhood tempt you to judge another person's spiritual journey. If words or thoughts of judgment find their way into your consciousness, I would gently but earnestly suggest that you immediately take them back. Bless the path of all who seek, and refuse to be afraid. Be grateful for your own unique and magical connection to the Divine. Release the idea once and for all that any one spiritual teacher, religion, or belief system has the only map leading back to Source.

ONE LAST LITTLE MESSAGE

The Universe is a magical place. It is always teaching us. Sometimes, it will lovingly, and even humorously, show us where we still have work to do.

The following is a true story. This literally happened as I was writing this final bit of the book.

I had just finished the paragraph above that begins "Tread lightly . . ." I knew the afterword wasn't complete, but I needed a break, so I ran to the grocery store. When I got into the car, a talk show I listen to was playing. The host was in the process of introducing a guest who *immediately* started saying that his religion was the only path to God and everything else was false. He began listing various ascended masters and called them "totally made up." Only *his* belief system was truth; all the rest would lead you straight to your end.

Of course, I found this to be either Universal irony or Heavenly humor. But as I listened to him, I found myself getting more and more annoyed. I wondered, *Why do people think this way? Why can't they just believe what they believe and leave everyone else alone?*

And then it hit me: *Oh, jeezle peats. I'm judging his judging. I'm judging the judger because he's being judgmental.*

That's when I started to laugh. Even as I finish this book about how there are infinite ways to the Divine, the Universe teaches me a lesson about how even the spiritual paths that think they're the only way still shouldn't be judged, even if they judge those of us who see things differently.

Oh, you goofy angels, you.

This, in turn, led me to wonder what the life lesson is for people who need the experience of a belief system where their way is the only way. What's all *that* about? (If I figure it out, I'll let you know.)

But this is what I'm talking about! This is what happens when you start talking to Source. This is what transpires if you reach upward and outward into the Universe, asking to learn.

If you listen, Divine guidance will come. This is what happens when you open yourself to the idea of a laughing, loving, and never-ending magical experience of life. All That Is will prove to you again and again that

Life is magic.

RECOMMENDED READING

The following are books on topics within each of the chapters of this compendium. Some are suitable for beginners, while others are best read once you've gotten a strong grasp of the fundamentals.

General Knowledge for a Magical Life

Conversations with God: Book One by Neale Donald Walsch

A Course in Miracles scribed by Helen Cohn Schucman, the Foundation for Inner Peace

Energy Strands: The Ultimate Guide to Clearing the Cords That Are Constricting Your Life by Denise Linn

Messages from Spirit: The Extraordinary Power of Oracles, Omens, and Signs by Colette Baron-Reid

The Magic of Angels

Angel Numbers 101: The Meaning of 111, 123, 444, and Other Number Sequences by Doreen Virtue

Angel Prayers: Harnessing the Help of Heaven to Create Miracles by Kyle Gray

Angelspeake: How to Talk with Your Angels by Barbara Mark and Trudy Griswold

Connecting with the Angels Made Easy: How to See, Hear, and Feel Your Angels by Kyle Gray

How to Be Your Own Genie: Manifesting the Magical Life You Were Born to Live by Radleigh Valentine

The Magic of Fairies

Fairies: Discover the Magical World of the Nature Spirits by Flavia Kate Peters

Fairies 101: An Introduction to Connecting, Working, and Healing with the Fairies and Other Elementals by Doreen Virtue

The Magic of Tarot and Oracle Cards

The Big Book of Angel Tarot by Radleigh Valentine

Tarot: A New Handbook for the Apprentice by Eileen Connolly

The Tarot Handbook by Hajo Banzhaf

The Tarot: History, Symbolism, and Divination by Robert M. Place

The Magic of Lenormand

The Complete Lenormand Oracle Handbook: Reading the Language and Symbols of the Cards by Caitlín Matthews

Lenormand Fortune Telling Cards by Harold Josten

The Magic of Runes

The Book of Runes by Ralph H. Blum

A Practical Guide to The Runes by Lisa Peschel

Taking Up the Runes: A Complete Guide to Using Runes in Spells, Rituals, Divination, and Magic by Diana L. Paxson

The Magic of Pendulums

Clear Home, Clear Heart: Learn to Clear the Energy of People and Places by Jean Haner

Dowsing: The Ultimate Guide for the 21st Century by Elizabeth Brown

Pendulum Magic For Beginners: Tap Into Your Inner Wisdom by Richard Webster

Pendulum Power: A Mystery You Can See, A Power You Can Feel by Greg Nielsen and Joseph Polansky

The Magic of the I Ching

The Complete I Ching: The Definitive Translation, 10th Anniversary Edition by Alfred Huang

I Ching: Or, The Book of Changes by James Legge

The I Ching or Book of Changes: A Guide to Life's Turning Points by Brian Browne Walker

The Magic of Astrology

The Complete Node Book: Understanding Your Life's Purpose by Kevin Burk

The Inner Sky: The Dynamic New Astrology for Everyone by Steven Forrest

Soul Signs: Harness the Power of Your Sun Sign and Become the Person You Were Meant to Be by Diane Eichenbaum

The Twelve Houses: Understanding the Importance of the Houses in Your Astrological Birthchart by Howard Sasportas

The Magic of Numerology

Your Hidden Symmetry: How Your Birth Date Reveals the Plan for Your Life by Jean Haner

Numerology: A Complete Guide to Understanding and Using Your Numbers of Destiny by Hans Decoz with Tom Monte

The Numerology Guidebook: Uncover Your Destiny and the Blueprint of Your Life by Michelle Buchanan

The Magic of Meditation

Meditation for Fidgety Skeptics: A 10% Happier How-to Book
by Dan Harris and Jeff Warren with Carlye Adler

Real Happiness: The Power of Meditation: A 28-Day Program
by Sharon Salzberg

*Secrets of Meditation: A Practical Guide to Inner Peace and Personal
Transformation* by davidji

Your 3 Best Superpowers: Meditation, Imagination, and Intuition
by Sonia Choquette

The Magic of Mantras

The Ancient Science of Mantras: Wisdom of the Sages
by Om Swami

*Healing Mantras: Using Sound Affirmations for Personal Power,
Creativity, and Healing* by Thomas Ashley-Farrand

Mantras: Words of Power by Swami Sivananda Radha

The 7 Secrets of Sound Healing by Jonathan Goldman

You Can Heal Your Life by Louise Hay

ACKNOWLEDGMENTS

If you have ever written a book, then you know it's a journey that no one takes alone. You may be the one at the keyboard, but there are others who make it all possible by supporting you in one way or another. And so, to that end, my deepest gratitude goes to:

My amazing guardian angels, who are always present and always with me: I'm certain that I regularly cause you to slap your foreheads in disbelief. Thank you, Joshua (and the others), for never giving up on me.

Archangels Uriel and Gabriel: It was 15 years ago when the golden glitter light of Archangel Uriel literally exploded into my life. Thank you for the epiphanies. Your presence in my life has transformed me. And dear Gabriel . . . always feeding me the perfect words for anything I'm writing or saying. Thank you so much.

Reid Tracy, Patty Gift, and Margarete Nielsen: For continuing to believe in me and providing unending support. Your faith in me is one of the greatest gifts in my life.

Louise Hay: Though you are gone now, we still feel you. You built a magical company where I can do my life's work and truly be myself. We love you and miss you.

Nicolette Salamanca Young: I don't even know how to express my gratitude to you. I'm completely convinced that you are the best editor in the world. Oh, and thank you for knowing me better than I know myself and *not* giving me that extension.

Sherry Warren: I know that this is the same thing I wrote in my last book for you, but honestly . . . it's too perfect. So once again, for keeping my head above water, for talking me off ledges, for fiercely protecting me, and for "the vault."

Colette Baron-Reid, Rebecca Campbell, Mike Dooley, Kyle Gray, John Holland, Denise Linn, and Dr. Christiane Northrup: One of the greatest gifts of being in the Hay House family is getting to learn from and become friends with amazing people like you. I am so honored to know you, to laugh with you, and to love you. A special thanks goes to all those in my mastermind group (and to Hay House for making that meeting possible). The advice you gave me quite literally changed my life! I am so grateful.

Nick C. Welch: The most amazing designer ever! Thank you for making my book pretty!

Mollie Langer, Christa Gabler, Greta Lipp, Nancy Grace Marder, and Mairead Conlon: For being the very best event producers on the planet—and then my friends. Thank you for always, *always* making me feel special.

Sharon Al-Shehab, Rocky George, Mike Joseph, Mitch Wilson, Steve Morris, and everyone at Hay House Radio: For making *Magical Things* truly magical and so much fun for me. You rock!

Curtis Donar, Jessica Polson, Laura Gray, Lindsay DiGianvittorio, Sarah Jaeger, McKenzie Pratt, Suzie Riker, and Kate Yen: For the magical opportunities, marketing, and internet support with my video courses. Teaching is my first love, and you all make that possible! (Also, thanks for making me look so good!)

Michelle Pilley, Jo Burgess, Julie Nolan, and the whole Hay House UK team: For always giving me a chance to sparkle.

To Lindsay McGinty and Richelle Fredson: For patiently teaching me all the PR stuff I am so clueless about!

Mary Lillibridge: For being the accountant so I don't have to, and for the lightning-fast responses.

Anna Grace Taylor, Anna Wolf, Erica Longdon, Liz Medhurst, and Polly Ford, my UK angels: Thank you for always being there for me and for all the prayers!

Lee Crump: For your love, your support, your faith in me—and for marrying me. I couldn't do this without you.

Raven, Jace, and Riley: For unending magic, laughter, and joy.

To my mom, Wanda Valentine: Even though you're not with us anymore, I feel your presence everyday. Thank you for teaching me the true meaning of faith.

Rhonda, Ted, Thaniel, and Keira Parolari; and Kristyn and Alex Bullard: For the love that can only come from family.

Dan Stone: For a lifelong friendship where no matter what I say or do, you just love me more. And ditto.

John Moore, kindred spirit and Disney BFF: In my heart, you will always be the one true Prince Phillip.

Mark Isley, Jeff Gurney, Mark Schaffer, Luc Beaudoin, Raphael Cordova, and Ben Wankel, my chosen family: I love you all so very much.

Valerie Camozzi, Susan Dintino, Eric Evangelista, Heather Hildebrand, Brigitte and Doug Parvin, and Robert Reeves, my angel family: For laughter and for endless prayers of support. I love you all!

Eric Grauberger: Because I can literally say *anything*, and it's totally safe.

Tanya Jahnke: For filling my home with magic and my heart with friendship. Love you, girl.

Chris Maher and Beth Urquhart: For weaving your magic into my magic so that I can have this life.

Kathy Azcuenaga, Pat Blocker, Kim Goehring, Dr. Julie Kelly, and Joan Ranquet: For making it possible for me to run all over the world knowing that my children are safe.

And finally, my students, the Certified Angel Tarot Readers and Certified Angel Card Readers: I have learned so much from you. I love our laughter and our serious talks and how amazingly compassionate you all are. Thank you for trusting me.

ABOUT THE
AUTHOR

Radleigh Valentine is a best-selling Hay House author of five tarot decks, one angel oracle card deck, and three books, including *The Big Book of Angel Tarot* and *How to Be Your Own Genie*. An internationally known spiritual teacher, he has spoken at more than 70 events in 10 countries since 2012, including over a dozen Hay House "I Can Do It" events. Radleigh is also a regular participant of the annual Hay House World Summit and is a frequent speaker at the Angel World Summit in London and Engelkongress in Germany and Austria.

Radleigh is the creator of the very popular Certified Angel Tarot Reader course. This online video class makes tarot easy through humor and expert insights that Radleigh has proven through teaching thousands of students. As a part of the class, Radleigh provides a private tutoring group that he monitors personally every day.

His Hay House Radio show, *Magical Things with Radleigh Valentine*, is a mixture of teaching through laughter and poignant readings for listeners. His very popular video show, *Ask Rad!*, streams on Facebook and Instagram simultaneously each week.

Find out more about Radleigh at www.radleighvalentine.com.

Hay House Titles of Related Interest

YOU CAN HEAL YOUR LIFE, the movie, starring Louise Hay & Friends
(available as a 1-DVD program, an expanded 2-DVD set,
and an online streaming video)
Learn more at www.hayhouse.com/louise-movie

THE SHIFT, the movie,
starring Dr. Wayne W. Dyer
(available as a 1-DVD program, an expanded 2-DVD set,
and an online streaming video)
Learn more at www.hayhouse.com/the-shift-movie

★ ✦ ★

LIGHT IS THE NEW BLACK: A Guide to Answering Your Soul's Callings
and Working Your Light, by Rebecca Campbell

MESSAGES FROM MARGARET: Down-to-Earth Angelic Advice for
the World . . . and You, by Gerry Gavin

MIRACLES NOW: 108 Life-Changing Tools for Less Stress, More Flow,
and Finding Your True Purpose, by Gabrielle Bernstein

RAISE YOUR VIBRATION: 111 Practices to Increase Your
Spiritual Connection, by Kyle Gray

YOU HAVE 4 MINUTES TO CHANGE YOUR LIFE: Simple 4-Minute
Meditations for Inspiration, Transformation, and True Bliss,
by Rebekah Borucki

All of the above are available at your local bookstore,
or may be ordered by contacting Hay House (see next page).

★ ✦ ★

We hope you enjoyed this Hay House book. If you'd like to receive our online catalog featuring additional information on Hay House books and products, or if you'd like to find out more about the Hay Foundation, please contact:

Hay House, Inc., P.O. Box 5100, Carlsbad, CA 92018-5100
(760) 431-7695 or (800) 654-5126
(760) 431-6948 (fax) or (800) 650-5115 (fax)
www.hayhouse.com® • www.hayfoundation.org

★✦★

Published in Australia by:
Hay House Australia Pty. Ltd., 18/36 Ralph St., Alexandria NSW 2015
Phone: 612-9669-4299 • *Fax:* 612-9669-4144 • www.hayhouse.com.au

Published in the United Kingdom by:
Hay House UK, Ltd., Astley House, 33 Notting Hill Gate, London W11 3JQ
Phone: 44-20-3675-2450 • *Fax:* 44-20-3675-2451 • www.hayhouse.co.uk

Published in India by: Hay House Publishers India,
Muskaan Complex, Plot No. 3, B-2, Vasant Kunj, New Delhi 110 070
Phone: 91-11-4176-1620 • *Fax:* 91-11-4176-1630 • www.hayhouse.co.in

★✦★

Access New Knowledge.
Anytime. Anywhere.

Learn and evolve at your own pace
with the world's leading experts.

www.hayhouseU.com

Hay House Podcasts
Bring Fresh, Free Inspiration Each Week!

Hay House proudly offers a selection of life-changing audio content via our most popular podcasts!

Hay House Meditations Podcast

Features your favorite Hay House authors guiding you through meditations designed to help you relax and rejuvenate. Take their words into your soul and cruise through the week!

Dr. Wayne W. Dyer Podcast

Discover the timeless wisdom of Dr. Wayne W. Dyer, world-renowned spiritual teacher and affectionately known as "the father of motivation." Each week brings some of the best selections from the 10-year span of Dr. Dyer's talk show on HayHouseRadio.com.

Hay House World Summit Podcast

Over 1 million people from 217 countries and territories participate in the massive online event known as the Hay House World Summit. This podcast offers weekly mini-lessons from World Summits past as a taste of what you can hear during the annual event, which occurs each May.

Hay House Radio Podcast

Listen to some of the best moments from HayHouseRadio.com, featuring expert authors such as Dr. Christiane Northrup, Anthony William, Caroline Myss, James Van Praagh, and Doreen Virtue discussing topics such as health, self-healing, motivation, spirituality, positive psychology, and personal development.

Hay House Live Podcast

Enjoy a selection of insightful and inspiring lectures from Hay House Live, an exciting event series that features Hay House authors and leading experts in the fields of alternative health, nutrition, intuitive medicine, success, and more! Feel the electricity of our authors engaging with a live audience, and get motivated to live your best life possible!

Find Hay House podcasts on iTunes, or visit www.HayHouse.com/podcasts for more info.